# LOOKING AT HERALDRY

By the same author

*The Romance of Heraldry*
*Civic Heraldry of England and Wales*
*Shakespeare's Heraldry*
*Boutell's Heraldry (revision)*
etc.

# LOOKING AT
# *HERALDRY*

*by*

### *C. W. Scott-Giles*
O.B.E., M.A., F.H.S.
FITZALAN PURSUIVANT OF ARMS EXTRAORDINARY

*With 153 Line Illustrations*

## PHOENIX HOUSE
## LONDON

Other books in the Excursions Series are GOING TO THE
CINEMA, by Andrew Buchanan (revised edition 1957 by
Stanley Reed); GOING TO THE THEATRE, by John
Allen; GOING TO THE BALLET, by Arnold Haskell;
GOING TO A CONCERT, by Lionel Salter; ENJOYING
BOOKS, by Geoffrey Trease; GOING TO LONDON, by
Anthony Weymouth (revised edition 1959 by Christopher
Trent); ENJOYING RADIO AND TELEVISION, by
Robert Dunnett; GOING TO MUSEUMS, by Jacqueline
Palmer; GOING INTO THE PAST, by Gordon J. Copley;
EXPLORING THE ROCKS, by Christopher Trent;
LOOKING AT THE STARS, by Michael W. Ovenden;
LOOKING AT BUILDINGS, by Christopher Trent;
ENJOYING JAZZ, by Rex Harris; EXPLORING THE
COUNTRYSIDE, by Christopher Trent.

© Text C. W. Scott-Giles 1962, 1966
Printed in Great Britain
by Lowe & Brydone (Printers) Ltd.
for J. M. DENT & SONS LTD
Aldine House · Bedford Street . London
A Phoenix House publication
First published 1962
Revised edition 1967

# CONTENTS

# ILLUSTRATIONS

# 1. How Heraldry Began

HERALDRY, rich in design and colour, is to be seen all around us—in churches, castles and manor-houses; on town halls, banks and other public buildings; on colleges and schools, and the blazer-pockets of their members; on flags and inn-signs and on the money we carry in our pockets. It is strange that something which is so widely used in decoration should be so little understood. Most people enjoy looking at some fine display of armorial bearings consisting of a splendid shield surmounted by a crested and mantled helm and per-haps supported by two fantastic creatures, and they may well wonder what it all means. Those who know something of heraldry find not only pleasure in its emblems and colour but also interest in reading their significance.

Unfortunately heraldry is generally thought to be a diffi-cult and rather obscure subject which can be understood only by those who take the trouble to master intricate rules and a language which at first sight is gibberish. In this book I hope to show that it is possible to learn enough about heraldry to

1

derive much interest from it without bothering too much about its grammar and rules. In some sections I shall deal with certain technicalities for readers who require them, but these can be passed over by others. (Heraldic terms are explained as they occur and are also included in the Index in *italics*.)

For the beginning of heraldry we must look back to the age of chivalry—that is, the period when armoured horsemen were the principal force in battle. Warriors armed in mail from head to foot looked very much alike and it was often difficult to tell one from another. How serious this might be is shown by an incident at the Battle of Hastings. A rumour spread among the Normans that Duke William had been slain. As the Bayeux Tapestry shows, there was nothing about his armour to indicate who he was, and like the other Norman warriors he was wearing a helm with a broad nose-piece which partly hid his face. Accordingly, to prove he was still alive, he had to push back his helm so that his followers could recognize his features.

To overcome this difficulty, in the second quarter of the twelfth century some knights began to use distinctive signs, or *cognizances*, by which they might be known when in armour. They had these signs painted on their shields and embroidered on the pennons which they carried on their lances. There was nothing new about painting devices on shields. The Greeks and Romans did so, and the Bayeux Tapestry shows some of the Normans at Hastings with wyverns or other creatures on their shields. What was new about the shield-devices introduced in the twelfth century was that they were adopted and systematically used not merely for decoration but for the practical purpose of distinguishing one armoured warrior from another, and also that they were passed down from father to son. They were borne both in war and at tournaments, where knights practised for war by competing in sword-play and jousting with lances, and their use spread rapidly when knights began to wear helms which completely covered their faces.

2. Seal of John de Warenne, Earl of Surrey, (c. 1235–1305).

As these signs were borne on arms they were called *armorial bearings*, or briefly *arms*. A shield with such a sign on it is a *shield of arms*. The surface of the shield is called the *field*, and the emblems placed or *charged* on it are called *charges*. Arms were displayed not only on shields but also on *banners*, which were rectangular flags originally of greater depth than width but later square. An early banner is shown in Fig. 1 and a square one in Fig. 81. Arms were also placed on the trappings of horses (Fig. 2). In the thirteenth century knights began to display their armorial bearings on the surcoats they wore over their armour for protection from rain and the sun's heat, and these were called their *coats of arms*. The term *coat of arms* (sometimes shortened to *coat*) is now often used when speaking of armorial bearings generally, whether they appear on surcoat, shield, banner, or some other article. As heraldry developed it was used more and more in the decoration of the knight's person and in the pageantry which accompanied tournaments.

From the first these personal signs had an important use apart from war and tournaments. A knight was not only a warrior: he was also a landholder and a man of business. As such he needed a seal for the purpose of signing documents. He had his name engraved on his seal, but as many people could not read the name he accompanied it by some distinc-

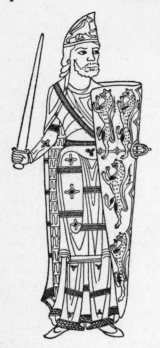

3. Geoffret 'Plantagenet', Count of Anjou, with the shield given him by Henry I in 1127.

4. Second Great Seal (1195) of King Richard I.

tive sign. When men began to paint cognizances on their shields they naturally used the same devices on their seals. Some seals bore little figures of their owners in armour and on horseback, and carrying a shield with their arms on it (Fig. 2). Others showed only the shield with its distinctive device. In this way a man's cognizance in war was also his signature in peace, and therefore doubly important to him, and it was natural that he should pass it on to his son. A young man, on growing to manhood and taking his part in war and tournament, would obviously wish to bear on his shield the same arms as his father used, though he had to make some minor change or addition to the arms to prevent confusion between him and his father. When the father died and the son succeeded to his lordship and estates he would clearly find it convenient to use on his seal the device which people already recognized as standing for that particular lordship. Consequently in three or four generations of consistent use, arms became something far more than a means of identifying the individual who bore them. They stood for a whole family and were its treasured possession. This was one reason why armorial bearings continued long after men ceased to carry shields and wear surcoats in war, and why heraldry has survived to the present day.

In England shields bearing cognizances made their appearance towards the end of Henry I's reign and their use increased in the reign of Stephen (1135–54). At the same time they were coming into use all over western Europe, and it is thought that the spread of the custom was largely due to knights of different countries meeting one another at tournaments. A prominent part in the organization of tournaments was taken by officers called *heralds*, who travelled through the country and even abroad to proclaim a forthcoming event, made the arrangements, announced the competitors, kept the score, declared the victors and marshalled the processions to and from the lists. Clearly the heralds must have found cognizances very useful in distinguishing between armoured men taking part in a tournament, and they made it their business to know the devices on the shields of as many knights as possible. As a result the heralds became the acknowledged experts in the system, and it was therefore called *heraldry*. The early heralds do not appear to have been in regular employment, but they travelled from place to place taking service with one lord after another for the period of a tournament. Later they became permanent officers in the household of a king or nobleman, or even an important knight, and they were given a variety of duties in connection with chivalry. The word *heraldry* strictly covers all the duties of heralds, and that part of them which had to do with devices on shields is sometimes called *armory*, but in these days most people think of heraldry as the art and system of armorial bearings, and the word is used with this meaning in this book.

The earliest shield of arms of which we have record is that which was given by the English King Henry I in 1127 to his son-in-law Geoffrey, Count of Anjou, who was called 'Plantagenet' from his habit of wearing a sprig of *planta genista*, or broom-plant. This shield, bearing a number of golden lions on a blue ground, appears on the effigy made after his death in 1151 (Fig. 3). As the illustration shows, he also had a lion on his cap, this too being gold on blue. Geoffrey's arms became hereditary, for his grandson William Longsword, Earl of Salisbury, bore a blue shield with six gold lions which may be seen on his tomb at Salisbury. The earliest seal bearing a shield of arms that has come down to us dates from about 1136. Thereafter the practice of using arms on shields and seals steadily increased, and by the first half of the thirteenth century it was the general custom among nobles and knights.

In addition to their arms some men wore distinctive ornaments, called *crests*, on the top of their helms. (The helm was not the mail or steel cap which an armoured man usually wore, but a metal headpiece put on over the cap when he went into battle or tournament.) An early example of a crest may be seen on the second Great Seal of Richard I, made in 1195 (Fig. 4). Here the crest takes the form of a fan-shaped plate with a lion painted on it like the ones in the King's shield. At first only kings and great nobles appear to have worn crests but early in the fourteenth century people of less importance adopted them. Early crests were small and light but later they became elaborate constructions of wood or moulded leather like those shown in Figs. 21 and 64. These great crests were probably used in tournaments and pageantry rather than in war because a man going into battle would be unlikely to put on his head something which would make him top-heavy. Not all knights in the days of chivalry adopted crests, but in modern times when a man obtains a grant of armorial bearings these nearly always include a crest as well as arms.

5. Thomas Beauchamp, Earl of Warwick, from his seal dated 1344.

A crest may consist of an emblem which appears in the shield, as in the case of Richard I, or it may be something quite different from the arms, as in Figs. 5 and 7. The junction of the crest and the helm was masked by a twisted scarf, called a *torse* or *crest-wreath* (as shown in Fig. 7), or by a decorated circlet called a *crest-coronet* (Fig. 82). The latter does not indicate any particular rank and must not be confused with a peer's coronet. In heraldic drawings the torse shows six twists which are alternately of one of the heraldic metals and colours listed in the next section, and usually those predominant in the arms. Falling from below the crest a knight wore a piece of material to prevent his helm getting unbearably hot in sunshine, and in heraldic art this has been developed into the decorative cloak which hangs down in folds and twists on each side of the shield. This is called the *mantling* or *lambrequin*. It is usually of one of the heraldic colours on the outside and lined with gold or silver, matching the tinctures of the shield, but in the case of the Royal Arms the mantling is gold lined with ermine.

How splendid a knight must have looked with his arms on his shield, surcoat and horse-trappings, and his crest on his helm, may be judged from the figure of Thomas de Beauchamp, third Earl of Warwick, drawn from a seal dated 1344 (Fig. 5). The field of his arms was red and the charges on it

B

were gold. The swan's head was white rising from a gold crest-coronet. Here the mantling is no more than a head-cloth covering the back of the helm, but if you look at Fig. 7 you will see the more elaborate type of mantling which developed from this.

A man's arms and crest were borne only by him personally and not by the soldiers who fought under his command. However, in addition to their arms and crests many nobles and knights had separate devices called *badges*, and these could be worn by their followers and retainers. Some badges were associated with particular lordships, and a man who had more than one lordship might have two or more badges.

6. Standard of Henry Bolingbroke, Duke of Lancaster.

He himself might wear one of these when he was not in armour, and he might use a badge as a mark of ownership on property and in other ways. In the fourteenth century some men included their badges, together with their arms and crests, in the designs on their seals, and if the badges consisted of some creature, like a lion or a dragon, two of them might be shown on the seal, one on each side of the shield. This was one of the things which in the following century led to the introduction of *supporters*—animals or birds, or sometimes human beings, placed on each side of the shield and shown holding it up. We are all familiar with the lion and the unicorn which are the supporters of the Royal Arms (see frontispiece).

Badges were sometimes displayed on long tapering flags

called *standards*, which also bore the cross of St George (or in Scotland the saltire of St Andrew). Fig. 6 shows the standard of Henry Bolingbroke, Duke of Lancaster (afterwards Henry IV) with his badges consisting of red roses of Lancaster, the white swan with a gold collar and chain of Bohun (his wife's family), and gold fox-tails and tree-stocks, all on a field parted white and blue, with the red cross of St George on white next to the staff. Standards were chiefly used in heraldic pageantry. Today the word standard is often misused. For example, the flag bearing the Royal Arms which flies over the place where the Sovereign is in residence is commonly referred to as the 'Royal Standard'. Being a rectangular flag it is properly described as the Royal Banner. It is important to use the correct terms when speaking of heraldic insignia, otherwise errors can arise. A common mistake is to refer to all armorial bearings indiscriminately as 'crests' or 'badges'. It may be helpful at this point to recapitulate the various parts of an *achievement of arms*—that is, a complete display of a person's heraldic insignia, and I take for this purpose a drawing of the armorial bearings of the Marquess of Abergavenny (Fig. 7).

The achievement consists of—

**The Arms**—a red shield bearing a white saltire (diagonal cross) and thereon a red rose. In heraldic terms this is, *Gules, on a saltire argent a rose gules*. These are the arms of the branch of the family of Nevill of which Lord Abergavenny is the head.

Above the shield is placed the coronet of a Marquess, and rising from this is a peer's helm on which is—

**The Crest**—a pied bull with a gold collar and attached thereto a gold chain turned over the bull's back.

The bull is standing on a *torse*, or *crest-wreath*, of six twists alternately white and red (these being the tinctures of the arms), and from under the torse falls the *mantling*, or *lambrequin*, which is red on the outside and lined with white.

7. Achievement of Arms of the Marquess
of Abergavenny.

**The Supporters**—the two pied bulls with gold collars and
chains flanking and upholding the shield.

**The Badges**—the red rose (of Lancaster) and the gold portcullis (of Beaufort), placed one on each side of the crest,
denoting Lord Abergavenny's descent from John of
Gaunt, Duke of Lancaster, by the family of Beaufort.

**The Motto**—on an escroll under the shield, is a usual accom-
paniment of armorial bearings. It will be noted that this
motto (translated as 'Form no mean wish') is a play on the
name of Nevill.

Most achievements of arms are simpler than this. Only
peers, a few baronets, knights of the Garter and knights of
the highest classes of the other orders of chivalry are entitled
to supporters. (Some corporate bodies, such as city councils,
also have supporters, but at the moment I am dealing only
with personal heraldry.) Many people who possess armorial
bearings have no badge. Consequently most achievements
consist only of the shield and crest with the accompanying
helm, crest-wreath, mantling and motto. The shield and
crest may be used independently, and you will frequently

see signet-rings or pieces of plate engraved with one or other of them. When the crest is used without the arms the helm and mantling are often omitted, but the crest-wreath or crest-coronet must be included.

Elaborate displays of arms, such as those of Lord Abergavenny, belong to the period when heraldry was fully developed, and when it had become a decorative art rather than a practical method of distinguishing one man from another. Early heraldry consisted primarily of the shield of arms. In the thirteenth century arms began to appear on the seals of men who could never have actually carried a shield in war or tournament, such as bishops and abbots. They had emblems, often of a religious character, on their seals. Following the example of nobles and knights they began to place these emblems on a shield, thereby creating arms which were eventually accepted as those of the see or abbey. Later the colleges at Oxford and Cambridge, the corporations of cities and towns and the companies of the City of London adopted arms for use on their seals and in other ways, and this resulted in the development of another kind of heraldry —corporate as distinct from personal and family heraldry. Today heraldry is very widely used by corporate bodies of all kinds.

## Heraldic Forms and Colours

The knightly shield varied in size and shape at different periods. On early thirteenth-century monuments shields extend from shoulder to knee, like that of Simon de Montfort, Earl of Leicester (Fig. 1). These large shields were carried in the days when body-armour consisted of mail—that is, interlinked iron rings. Towards the end of the thirteenth century shields became rather smaller, and this tendency increased in the following century when knights began to strengthen their mail with plate armour on the upper arms and shins. In the fifteenth century, when complete plate armour was introduced, the shield was rarely carried except at tournaments. Heraldic shields used in pageantry and decoration then became ornamental rather than practical, and in later times they were given all sorts of fantastic shapes which would have been impossible for a knight to carry. In the present century heraldic artists have returned to the simple form of shield borne in the days of chivalry, and this is used in the illustrations in this book. In heraldic drawings shields may be placed upright or aslant according to the taste of the artist.

Arms on shields were at first simple in design and bold in colour so as to be clearly visible at a distance on the battlefield or in the lists. The choice of colour was of great practical importance. It was found that a silver charge on a gold field, or a red one on blue, would not show up so well as blue on silver or gold on red. Accordingly knights were careful to have their shields painted in contrasting hues. A distinction was drawn between *metals*, i.e. gold and silver (often represented by yellow and white), and *colours*, i.e. red, blue, green, purple and black. To ensure the visibility of arms it became the practice to avoid placing a metal charge on a metal field, or a charge of one colour on a field of another colour. There were exceptions to this. For instance, if the field were partly metal and partly colour—say gold and green—it was permissible to place on it a charge of another colour—say a red lion. The test was whether the charges would show up well against their background. Notwithstanding various exceptions it became a general principle not to place metal on metal or colour on colour, and this is still followed.

In addition to the metals and colours of heraldry there are a number of *furs*, which are represented by conventional designs. The furs were originally ermine, shown by black tails, or 'spots', on a white ground; and vaire, consisting of alternate white and blue shield-shaped pieces standing for the skins of grey squirrels. Variations of these were introduced later.

Metals, colours and furs are collectively termed *tinctures*. Several of the tinctures have special heraldic names, for which there are recognized abbreviations used in written descriptions of arms. In the seventeenth century a system was devised by which tinctures could be indicated in uncoloured drawings of arms by dots and hatching lines, and this is often used when arms are engraved on gold and silver plate, or shown in some other form where it is not possible to use colour. This system of hatching is illustrated in Fig 11 but I have not employed it generally in this book.

The following table gives the various tinctures, their heraldic names and abbreviations, and the way in which they may be indicated by hatching:

| | *Heraldic Name* | *Represented thus :* |
|---|---|---|
| *Metals* | | |
| Gold (or yellow) | *Or* or *Gold* | |
| Silver (or white) | *Argent* (abbreviated *Arg.*) | |
| *Colours* | | |
| Blue | *Azure* (abbreviated *Az.*) | |
| Red | *Gules* (abbreviated *Gu.*) | |
| Green | *Vert* | |
| Purple | *Purpure* (abbreviated *Purp.*) | |
| Black | *Sable* (abbreviated *Sa.*) | |
| *Furs* | | |
| Represented by white and blue pieces unless otherwise stated | *Vaire* *Potent* | |
| White with black tufts | *Ermine* | |
| Black with white tufts | *Ermines* | |
| Gold with black tufts | *Erminois* | |
| Black with gold tufts | *Pean* | |

(Instead of *ermines*, *erminois* and *pean* you may say *sable ermined argent*, *gold ermined sable*, and *sable ermined or*.)

Party fields     Ordinaries     Diminutives     Varied fields

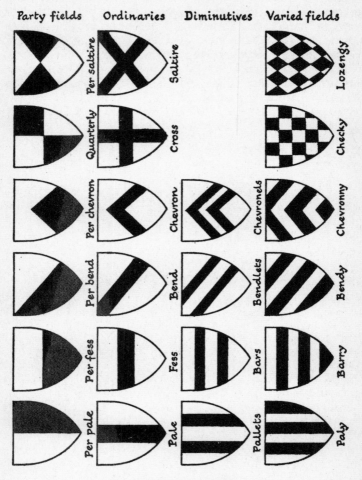

Per saltire — Saltire — — Lozengy

Quarterly — Cross — — Checky

Per chevron — Chevron — Chevronels — Chevronny

Per bend — Bend — Bendlets — Bendy

Per fess — Fess — Bars — Barry

Per pale — Pale — Pallets — Paly

8. Simple forms and fields.

There are certain shades of colour and variations of the furs which are not included in this list because they are seldom seen.

Objects represented in heraldry in their natural or proper colours are described as *proper* (abbreviated *ppr*).

The simplest arms were produced by drawing a line across the middle of the shield—vertically, horizontally or diagonally—and painting the two halves in different tinctures. For instance, the shield of the family of Waldegrave is *party* (i.e. divided) vertically, the dexter side being white and the sinister side red. Here it must be noted that the words *dexter* and *sinister* applied to the right and left sides of the shield are from the point of view of the man bearing the shield in front of him; therefore when you look at a shield the dexter is on your left and the sinister is on your right. This also applies to the other parts of an achievement, so that in the Royal Arms (see frontispiece) the lion is the dexter supporter and the unicorn is the sinister supporter.

Some old arms consist only of a broad stripe painted down or across the middle of the shield. A vertical stripe is called a *pale*, a horizontal one a *fess*, a diagonal downward from dexter to sinister a *bend*, and one along the other diagonal a *bend sinister*. Other simple forms are the *chevron* (normally shown with its point upwards), the *cross*, the *saltire* (a cross set diagonally), and the *chief* (a broad bar across the top of the shield). These forms are called *ordinaries* because they are so commonly found in arms, either alone or with other charges.

The pale, fess, bend, chevron, cross, and saltire are illustrated in the second row of Fig. 8. If you look at the first row you will see how *party fields* are formed by divisions along the lines of these ordinaries. Thus a shield divided by a vertical line is described as *party per pale* or *party palewise*; by a horizontal line, *party per fess* or *party fesswise*, etc. (The word *party* is often omitted.)

The ordinaries may occupy up to a third of the depth or width of the shield. You cannot have two pales, two fesses, etc., on a shield, but some of these ordinaries have a narrower form (known as its diminutive) with a special name, as shown in the third row of Fig. 8, and two or three or more of these diminutives can be included in the same design.

The fourth row shows *varied fields* produced by an odd number of parallel lines so as to make an even number of divisions, and these fields are described as *paly*, *barry*, *bendy* and *chevronny* according to the direction of the lines. Six divisions are shown in the illustrations, but there could be four, eight,

Formy        Patonce        Flory        Potent

Moline        Maltese        Pommy        Crosslet

9. Some heraldic crosses.

ten or twelve. Intersecting lines, crosswise and saltirewise, make *checky* and *lozengy*. The cross and saltire are not narrowed to form diminutives, but small crosses and saltires are found as charges in arms. The cross is a popular charge, due to its Christian significance, and is found in many forms, some of which are shown in Fig. 9.

Some arms consisted of an ordinary on a party or varied field. For example, Geoffrey Chaucer, whose arms may be seen on his tomb in Westminster Abbey, bore a shield parted palewise argent and gules and thereon a bend counterchanged—that is, the bend is red where it lies on the white half of the field, and white on the 1ed half (Fig. 11). It was possible to produce a large number of different shields of arms simply by combining fields divided in various ways with a number of geometrical forms. Further variety was obtained by making the dividing lines or the edges of the ordinaries wavy or zig-zag instead of straight. For example, the banner of Hinckley carried by Simon de Montfort (Fig. 1) is divided by a vertical zig-zag (or *dancetty*) line into

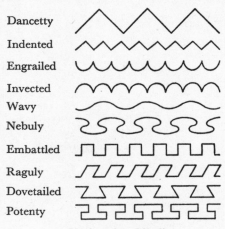

| | |
|---|---|
| Dancetty | |
| Indented | |
| Engrailed | |
| Invected | |
| Wavy | |
| Nebuly | |
| Embattled | |
| Raguly | |
| Dovetailed | |
| Potenty | |

10. Various heraldic lines.

white and red. The various kinds of lines used in heraldry, with their descriptions, are shown in Fig. 10.

Instances of arms consisting only of various kinds of lines and shapes combined in different designs and colours are given in Fig. 11, where the tinctures are indicated by hatching and the description in heraldic terms is given below the drawings. (The language of heraldry is dealt with in the next chapter.) You may think arms of this sort rather uninteresting as compared with a shield containing a spirited lion or some grotesque creature like a dragon, but you must remem-

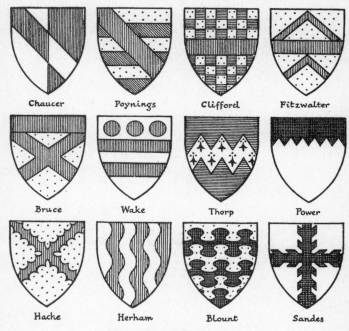

11. Some simple shields of arms.

The following are the heraldic descriptions of the above arms. In each case the field is described first. The name of the tincture follows the charge to which it refers.

*Chaucer:* Per pale argent and gules, a bend counterchanged.

*Poynings:* Barry of six or and vert, a bend gules.

*Clifford:* Checky or and azure, a fess gules.

*Fitzwalter:* Or, a fess between two chevronels gules.

(The word gules refers back to all the charges mentioned since the first tincture and therefore applies to the chevronels.)

*Bruce:* Or, a saltire and a chief gules.

*Wake:* Argent, two bars and in chief three roundles gules.

*Thorp:* Azure, a fess dancetty ermine.

*Power:* Argent, a fess indented sable.

*Hache:* Or, a saltire engrailed gules.

(Note that an *engrailed* line has the points outwards. When the points are inwards it is *invected*.)

*Herham:* Paly wavy of six argent and gules.

*Blount:* Barry nebuly of six or and sable.

*Sandes:* Argent, a cross raguly sable.

ber that the original purpose of heraldry was to provide warriors with distinctive marks, and a plain or party shield with a bend or cross or chevron painted on it served this purpose just as well as something more picturesque. However, from the first some knights showed rather more imagination in their choice of arms and included beasts, birds, fishes or flowers in their shields, and as heraldry developed very many natural and artificial objects were introduced. Some of these are described in the next chapter.

12. Lion rampant.    13. Crowned lion    14. Lions passant.
                         rampant.

# 2. Heraldic Signs and Wonders

ANYTHING under the sun may form part of armorial bearings.
Indeed that is an understatement, because the sun itself and
some of the constellations are found as charges on shields,
while the imagination of the heralds has produced some
creatures unknown to the realm of nature. In the twelfth and
thirteenth centuries knights placed on their shields a number
of things in addition to the simple forms dealt with in the
last chapter, but at first their choice was not very wide.
Animals found in the arms of this period include lions, bears
and hounds, together with the heads of boars, stags and
wolves, and also fabulous creatures such as the dragon and
the griffin. Among birds we find eagles, ravens, falcons,
herons and popinjays (or parrots), and fish are represented
by dolphins, pike and salmon. Certain floral forms such as
fleurs-de-lis, roses and cinquefoils are common, and everyday objects found in early shields of arms include gauntlets,
buckles, trumpets and horns, cups, ladies' sleeves, scallop-
shells and water-budgets (leather bottles for carrying water).

Very early in the development of heraldry some men with
names which could be put into picture form chose emblems
illustrating or playing on their surname. For instance, William Heron had a heron on his shield, and a knight named

de Kenetz bore three kennets (hunting dogs). These *allusive arms* (as they are called) had a practical value because they were readily associated with their owners and easily remembered, and they became very popular. Many new charges were introduced into heraldry for the purpose of representing surnames in pictorial form. Thus Nichole de la Hose placed on his shield three men's hose, Thomas Trevett chose a trivet, Robert de Bowes three longbows, and so on. It is interesting to look for such punning allusions to names, but to detect them you must sometimes think of the French or Latin word for the charge in the shield. To see the pun in the

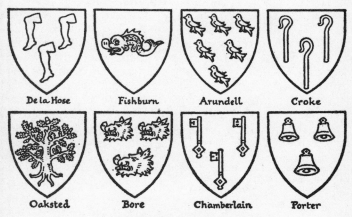

15. Arms allusive to names and offices.

The following are the heraldic descriptions of the above arms:

*De la Hose:* Argent, three men's hose gules.
*Fishburn:* Gules, a dolphin argent.
*Arundell:* Sable, six martlets (or hirondelles) argent.
*Croke:* Azure, three gold crooks.
*Oaksted:* Argent, an uprooted oak tree proper.
*Bore:* Azure, three boars' heads or.
*Chamberlain:* Azure, three gold keys erect.
*Porter:* Sable, three silver bells.

six swallows borne by the Arundell family you must remember that the French for swallow is *hirondelle*. Similarly there are hammers (*martels*) in the arms of Martel, hedgehogs (*hérissons*) in those of Herries, and a bear (*ursus*) in those of FitzUrse. Some knights whose surnames were taken from offices which they held chose arms referring to their duties. William le Chamberlain bore three keys, and Allayne Boteler (or Butler) three cups on his shield. These are only a few instances of a large number of allusive arms. Examples are given in Fig. 15.

Except for such references to names and offices, heraldry in the age of chivalry seldom held any inner meaning, but armorial bearings granted in Tudor and later times often contained emblems alluding to the deeds and careers of those on whom they were conferred. This is still the case, and if you look at the arms of peers and baronets in a modern Peerage you will see some animals, flowers and objects which were unknown when heraldry began, such as kangaroos and flamingoes, sugar-bush flower and mimosa, cycle-wheels, miners' safety-lamps and even a telescope. Charges of this kind are frequent in the arms of towns—for instance, Swindon has a railway locomotive and Beddington-and-Wallington an aeroplane in its shield. Some people find it incongruous that modern inventions should have a place in an ancient and traditional art, but if every object which did not exist in the days of chivalry had been excluded from heraldry it would have become a static art, and a thing of the past, instead of one which is constantly developing and keeping in touch with the times. The heralds have sometimes shown much ingenuity in using traditional forms to represent the latest scientific developments. For example, the arms of the United Kingdom Atomic Energy Authority (Fig. 145) convey the idea of nuclear fission in an atomic pile by a design consisting entirely of forms found in early heraldry. These are described in Chapter 10.

The heavenly bodies became charges in arms at an early date. In the time of Edward I a gold sun on a blue shield

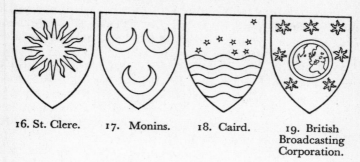

16. St. Clere.    17. Monins.    18. Caird.    19. British
                                                  Broadcasting
                                                  Corporation.

(Fig. 16) was borne by John de St Clere, probably with a
clear sky in mind, just as in later times a family named Fair-
weather had a sun and three stars in their arms. As an
emblem of royal majesty the sun was used as a badge by
Richard II and some of his successors. The moon is not frequently depicted in heraldry, but the crescent is a common
charge and sometimes represents the moon, as in the punning
arms of Monins—three gold crescents on red (Fig. 17). Stars
appear in two forms. When they have wavy rays they are
called *estoiles*, and these may be seen in Fig. 19. Stars with
straight rays are termed *molets* or *mullets* (from *molette*, a spur-
rowel) and are common charges. Groups of stars representing
particular constellations are sometimes found in modern
heraldry. Sir James Caird, the shipowner, was granted arms
containing the seven stars forming the Great Bear together
with the North Star, gold upon blue, the lower part of the
shield being wavy silver and blue signifying the sea (Fig. 18).
The Southern Cross appears on the shield of Lord Birdwood
of Anzac. The arms of the British Broadcasting Corporation
consist of a blue shield bearing within seven silver estoiles
the earth encircled by a gold ring which stands for world-
embracing radio transmissions (Fig. 19). The earth also
forms part of the crest of the family of Hope. Here it is
depicted with a great rent in its side as though broken by
some devastating explosion, while above it is a rainbow be-
c

tween clouds, the meaning of the design being pointed by the accompanying motto, *At spes infracta*—'Yet Hope is unbroken'. This is not a medieval crest, but belongs to the symbolic heraldry of the seventeenth century.

From the beginning of heraldry the animal most frequently found in arms was the lion, because it was regarded as the king of beasts and also as typifying the strength and courage of a warrior. Several kings and princes had lions on their shields. The kings of Scotland, Norway and Leon each displayed one lion, while the king of Denmark had three and the princes of North Wales four. In England Richard I, the 'Lion-heart', bore three lions on his shield from 1195, and there is reason to believe that a lion was a royal badge as early as the reign of Henry I. The lion was not restricted to the royal house and families connected with it. Many knights had lions painted on their shields to show how strong and fierce they were—or wanted people to think they were. Indeed so many men wished to bear a lion that to make their arms sufficiently distinctive they had to show the animal in different attitudes. In early heraldry the lion was shown standing erect on one hind paw with the other paws raised. This is now known as a *lion rampant* (Fig. 12). A different heraldic charge was produced by showing the lion walking with the right forepaw raised, when he was described as a *lion passant* (Fig. 14). Further variations were introduced by turning the lion's head so that he looked out of the shield (when he was called *gardant*), or over his back (*regardant*). The lion might also be given a forked tail, as in the arms of Simon de Montfort (Fig. 1), whose lion was white on a red field. Again, the lion might be crowned (Fig. 13), or collared, or charged on the shoulder with some small object—details which served to make each one distinctive so that no two knights bearing this popular beast should have exactly the same arms. The early heralds were not very clear about the difference between a lion and a leopard. They regarded a lion prowling and looking sideways as behaving like a leopard. That is why the beasts in the English Royal Arms are sometimes described as leopards, though they are never shown with spots. Nowadays they are called *lions passant gardant* (Fig. 23 and Table I).

The heraldic lion is not much like the natural animal. It was probably first drawn from hearsay by men who had never seen a real lion, and they produced a creature symbolic of ferocious strength rather than true to nature. Figs. 12–14 are fine examples of the lion of heraldry. Fig. 12 is from the seal of Sir Henry Percy, Lord of Alnwick (*d.* 1315), whose arms were a blue lion rampant on gold. Fig. 13 shows the shield of Richard, Earl of Cornwall (1209–72) in Westminster Abbey. The lion is red with a gold crown on a white field within a black border charged with golden roundels. Fig. 14 shows the arms of John, Lord Strange (*d.* 1397) in Canterbury Cathedral. The lions are white on red. In the nineteenth century heraldic artists often drew lions closely resembling the real animal, but these appeared tame in comparison with medieval examples, and today the stylized lion of early heraldry is usually shown in arms.

Many other animals were soon found in heraldry, including deer of all kinds, horses and hounds, oxen, sheep and goats, bears, boars, wolves, foxes and badgers, and as these were familiar to those who painted shields they were shown more or less true to nature. On the other hand creatures which were known only from travellers' tales were given an imaginative form. The tiger was drawn like a lion but with a down-curving tusk on the end of its nose. The antelope had jagged horns (Fig. 66) and sometimes tusks, and the panther was covered with spots of various colours and was generally *incensed*—that is, having flames coming from its mouth and ears. These three animals are also found in their natural forms in modern heraldry. Some creatures were given unusual names. The giraffe was called a camelopard because it was thought to be a cross between a camel and a leopard, and the elephant is sometimes known by the old form *olifaunt*. Its head forms a punning crest of the Oliphant family.

20. Dragon.          21. Wyvern crest          22. Griffin.
                     of Sir John Gray
                     on his Garter stall-
                     plate.

The fabulous creatures of heraldry are termed *monsters*—a word which means unnatural and not necessarily huge. Those most frequently found are the *dragon*, a scaly four-legged creature with claws and bat-like wings (Fig. 20); the *wyvern*, which is like a dragon but has only two legs (Fig. 21); the *griffin*, which has the head, wings and claws of an eagle, and the body, hind-legs and tail of a lion (Fig. 22); and the *unicorn*, which has a horse's head and mane together with a beard and one twisted horn projecting from the forehead, the body and hoofs being like those of a deer and the tail that of a lion. A red dragon has come down to us from antiquity as the badge of Wales, and was one of the supporters of the Royal Arms in Tudor times. The unicorn is familiar as the Scottish supporter of the present Royal Arms (see frontispiece), but it is not an exclusively Scottish emblem and is found in the heraldry of some English families. The heads of all these creatures are also found as charges in arms.

The *yale* is a deer-like creature with horns curving in opposite directions, which it was supposed to be able to swivel round. It is often represented with spots on the body. The yale was a badge of the Beaufort family (descended from John of Gaunt, Duke of Lancaster), and it may be seen at Westminster Abbey on the tomb of Lady Margaret Beaufort,

King Henry III.     The Emperor     King Edward
                    Frederick II.   the Confessor.

23. Ancient shields in Westminster Abbey.

mother of Henry VII. Yales also appear as supporters of her arms at Christ's and Saint John's Colleges at Cambridge, of which she was the Foundress (Fig. 98).

Among other fabulous creatures found in heraldry are the *pegasus* (or winged horse), the *sea-lion*, consisting of the head and fore-quarters of a lion joined to a fish's tail, the *triton* (or merman), and the *mermaid*. There are also some monsters which are mentioned in books on heraldry but are very seldom found in arms. One of these is the *enfield*, which has a fox's head, a lion's body, an eagle's claws and a wolf's hind legs and tail. This remarkable hybrid was rarely seen until the Enfield (Middlesex) Urban District Council obtained armorial bearings in 1945 and chose this monster for their arms.

The eagle was regarded as chief among birds as the lion was among beasts, and like the lion it was given an heraldic form not much like that of nature. It is usually shown *displayed*—that is, with its wings spread out on each side of its body. As a symbol of ancient Rome the eagle was associated with imperial rule, and it became the emblem of the Holy Roman Empire of the middle ages. The arms of the Empire, a black eagle on gold, may be seen among the shields set up in Westminster Abbey by Henry III (Fig. 23). Here the eagle has one head (which is damaged), but in later representations of these arms it has two heads, said to symbolize the jurisdiction of the Emperor over both eastern and western

Europe. When Mary I married Philip II of Spain (son of the Emperor Charles V), the black eagle became for a short time one of the supporters of the English Royal Arms. The eagle was used as an emblem by other rulers besides the Emperor, including Edward III, who had an eagle among his badges. It also became a general charge in heraldry and is found in the arms of many men in no way connected with royalty. In religious heraldry the eagle is the emblem of St John the Divine.

The pelican also takes an heraldic rather than a natural form. Three silver pelicans on blue are the arms of the Pelham family (Fig. 50) and were no doubt suggested by the surname. The pelican is often shown wounding its breast with its beak and drawing blood with which to feed its young. This is a symbol of the Holy Eucharist, and pelicans so represented are said to be 'in their piety'. Two such pelicans, white on a red field, are found in the arms of Corpus Christi College, Cambridge (Fig. 100).

It is natural that so familiar and beautiful a bird as the swan should be frequently seen in heraldry. It is found as a charge on the shield, a crest, a badge and a supporter. A swan's head and neck forming a crest is shown in Fig. 5. As a badge the swan appears on the banner of Henry Bolingbroke (Fig. 6), who derived it from his wife, Mary Bohun. The Dukes of Buckingham, also descended from the Bohun family, similarly used the swan as a badge, and from them it has come down as a county emblem in Buckinghamshire (Fig. 129).

Hawks, herons, storks, ostriches, ravens and crows are among the birds often seen in heraldry, and in many cases they allude to the names of those who bear them. Thus a corbie (or crow) is found in the arms of the family of Corby and in the crest of the Northamptonshire town of Corby, while the Falconers bear falcons and the Starkies storks. A peacock with its tail spread is said to be 'in its pride', while a crane 'in its vigilance' is shown standing on one leg and holding a stone in the lifted claw, so that if it falls asleep it will wake itself by dropping the stone.

24. Lucy.    25. Scales.    26. Earls of Chester.

A very common heraldic charge is the *martlet*, which is usually represented without legs and sometimes without a beak. This cannot be identified with any particular bird of nature, but typifies birds like martins and swallows, the absence of legs arising from the idea that these birds never land on the ground. The punning *hirondelles* in the arms of the Arundell family are often drawn as martlets (Fig. 15). In the arms of Westminster Abbey (Fig. 85) the martlets represent doves, being derived from the shield associated with Edward the Confessor (Fig. 23). He in fact lived before the days of heraldry, but when Henry III rebuilt the Abbey and had the arms of its benefactors carved on the walls, a shield was devised to represent the Confessor as its founder. This was blue with a gold cross patonce between five gold doves, and was based on the design on one of the Confessor's coins. In the shield of the Abbey the Confessor's arms appear with martlets instead of doves, and accompanied by a gold chief bearing the old Royal Arms between Tudor roses.

Heads and wings of birds occur as charges in arms, and also feathers. Most people are familiar with the badge known as 'the Prince of Wales's feathers', consisting of three ostrich plumes passing through a coronet and accompanied by the motto *Ich dien* ('I serve'). An ostrich feather was one of the badges of Edward III and was used in various forms by several of his descendants. The three feathers are associated particularly with his eldest son, Edward, Prince of Wales,

27. Old Arms of       28. Boscawen.          29. Bardolph.
    France.

who bore three separate feathers on a black field as his
'shield for peace', shown on his tomb at Canterbury. (His
'shield for war' bore his father's arms with a white label
appropriate to the eldest son.) Edward's nickname, 'the
Black Prince', was derived from the sable shield and surcoat
on which the ostrich plumes were displayed.

The dolphin takes an heraldic form which is shown in the
arms of Fishburn (Fig. 15). Fish were frequently chosen in
allusion to names. The Lucy family bore three silver luces
(or pike) on a red shield strewn with silver cross-crosslets
(Fig. 24), and families named Herring, Salmon and Trout-
beck have the appropriate fish in their arms. Whelk shells are
borne by Shelly, and six silver scallop shells on red are the
arms of Scales (Fig. 25). The scallop shell, or *escallop*, has
been a common charge from early times because it is the
emblem of St James, patron of pilgrims, and they wore it as a
badge. Snakes are also found in arms, and in modern heraldry
the rod of Aesculapius—a staff entwined by a serpent—is an
emblem of healing and has been included in the arms of members of the medical profession. Insects are rare in old shields of
arms, but in the course of time have become more common. A
grasshopper is shown in Fig. 140. The bee occurs as an emblem of industry in the arms of several manufacturing towns,
and in some family arms in allusion to the name. Earl

Beatty of the North Sea was granted a blue shield charged with a gold beehive surrounded by nine gold bees, and on a white chief the red cross of St George appropriate to an Admiral of the Fleet.

Trees and plants of many kinds, and their leaves and fruit, are found in heraldry, sometimes with reference to names. The tree of Paradise with the Serpent twined about its trunk and Adam and Eve standing beside it appears in the arms of the Fruiterers Company of the City of London. The oak in which Charles II hid after the Battle of Worcester is a charge in the shield granted to Colonel Carlos, who shared the hiding-place (Fig. 55). Three red apples on a white shield are the arms of Applegarth, and the crest of Perrott is doubly allusive to the name, being a parrot holding a pear. The wheatsheaf (called by the old French word *garb*) has been a common charge from early times. Three gold wheatsheaves on blue were the arms of the Earls of Chester (Fig. 26) and are found in the shields of the City of Chester (Fig. 127), the Cheshire County Council and several towns in the county.

Fleurs-de-lis, roses and cinquefoils are the commonest floral forms in heraldry, though many other flowers are also found. A blue shield strewn with gold fleurs-de-lis was the old Royal Arms of France (Fig. 27), and the fleur-de-lis also has royal associations in England because the English sovereigns from Edward III to George III incorporated the arms of France in their shields, as shown in Chapter 6. The fleur-de-lis is also in general heraldic use and appears in the shields of many families unconnected with royalty. The rose usually takes the conventional form illustrated in Fig. 28, where it is red on an ermine field. As a badge the rose is seen on the standard of Henry Bolingbroke (Fig. 6). Here is it the red rose of Lancaster which opposed the white rose of York in the struggle called 'the Wars of the Roses'. Henry VII united the roses, and a red rose with a white centre is still the Royal Badge for England. The cinquefoil, which may be seen in Fig. 29 (Azure, three gold cinquefoils), is a conventional flower of five petals.

Barnacles    Bird-bolts    Bugle-horn    Caltraps

Chessrooks    Clarions    Covered Cups    Cushions

Escarbuncle    Maunch    Pheon    Water Budgets

30. Some common heraldic charges.

The following are the bearers and the heraldic descriptions of the above arms:

*Barnake:* Argent, three horse-barnacles sable.
*Boson:* Argent, three bird-bolts gules, heads sable.
*Hornacot:* Gules, a bugle-horn or.
*Trappes:* Argent, three caltraps sable.
*Rooke:* Sable, three chess-rooks argent.
*Granville:* Argent, three clarions gules.
*Boteler* (or *Butler*): Azure, three gold cups with covers.
*Becard:* Argent, three lozenge-shaped cusions (or oreillers) gules.
*Haltham:* Azure, an escarbuncle or.
*Hastings:* Or, a maunch (sleeve) gules.
*Sidney:* Or, a pheon azure.
*Trusbut:* Argent, three water-budgets gules.

Objects found as charges in heraldry are far too numerous to list and illustrate in this book, but Fig. 30 shows a number of things which frequently appear in arms and have distinctive heraldic forms. For these examples, and those given in Fig. 15, I have chosen arms consisting either of a single object or a group of similar objects on a plain field. However, many charges were placed on party or varied fields, or were borne in the same shield as one of the ordinaries. Charges might be placed on an ordinary, or an ordinary might be placed between a number of charges. In some rather more complicated shields we find ordinaries placed between charges and with other charges upon them. Examples are given in Figs. 31 and 32. The descriptions in heraldic terms of the arms shown in these figures are given below them.

If you consider these illustrations you will see that a knight wishing to adopt arms had all sorts of alternatives open to him. The field might be of one tincture throughout, or it might be party or varied, and the dividing lines might be straight or wavy, indented, etc.; or the field might be *semy* (or scattered) with crosslets or fleurs-de-lis or other small objects. There were the ordinaries and their diminutives to choose from, and these also might have straight or ornamental edges. There were also innumerable other charges, and these might be borne singly or in groups, and with one of the ordinaries. Finally there was the range of metals, colours and furs from which to select. Obviously a very large number of different shields of arms could be produced by combining these different elements of design.

I have referred to knights adopting or choosing their arms because in the early days of heraldry there was no formal granting of arms by recognized authorities as there is today. Knights devised arms for themselves, taking care not to choose the same combination of design and colour as someone else already had on his shield. Certain things influenced their choice. I have already mentioned the popularity of playing on one's name, though not everyone with a name having pictorial possibilities chose allusive arms. Some knights chose

Greystoke        Gascoigne        Vernon

Camoys        Stanley        Cobham

31. The following are the heraldic descriptions of the above arms:

*Greystoke:* Barry of six argent and azure, three chaplets gules.

*Gascoigne:* Argent, on a pale sable a conger's head or.

*Vernon:* Or, on a fess azure three gold garbs.

*Camoys:* Or, on a chief gules three roundles argent.

*Stanley:* Argent, on a bend azure three bucks' faces with antlers or.

*Cobham:* Gules, on a chevron or three estoiles sable.

Howard          Berkeley          De la Pole

Erpingham          Bourchier          Guildeford

**32.** The following are the heraldic descriptions of the above arms:

*Howard:* Gules, a bend between six cross-crosslets fitchy (i.e. having their lower limbs pointed) argent.

*Berkeley:* Gules semy of crosslets formy, a chevron argent.

*De la Pole:* Azure, a fess between three leopards' faces or.

*Erpingham:* Vert, an inescutcheon within an orle of martlets argent.

*Bourchier:* Argent, a cross engrailed gules between four water-budgets sable.

*Guildeford:* Or, a saltire between four martlets sable.

a design resembling, though distinct from, the arms of their feudal overlord; for example the Vernons (Fig. 31) based their arms on those of the Earls of Chester (Fig. 26) from whom they held their land.

It sometimes happened that two knights accidentally chose the same arms, and the duplication was only discovered when they met—or perhaps only when their sons or grandsons met and found they were bearing identical shields. At the siege of Caerlaverock Castle in Scotland in 1300, Brian Fitzalan and Hugh Pointz both had shields barry gold and red, which led to a dispute between them. When such duplication of arms came to light, if neither man bearing the arms was willing to adopt a different shield the case was referred to the Court of Chivalry presided over by the Constable and the Marshal. The most famous case which came before this court was in the reign of Richard II, when three men—Sir Richard Scrope, Sir Robert Grosvenor, and a Cornish squire named Carminow—were all found to be bearing a gold bend on a blue shield. After prolonged proceedings it was decided that Scrope had the right to the arms, and the others had to take different shields.

It is rather surprising that there were not more cases of duplication at a time when men chose arms for themselves, and when there was no register to which they could refer to see whether the design they had in mind was already in use. While we do not know much about the activities of the heralds at that time, it seems probable that knights would turn to them for information and advice in the choice of arms. It may well be that some of the heralds noted down the shields that came to their notice so as to be in a position to advise knights on the designs they might choose without the risk of infringing on some existing arms. We know that by the middle of the thirteenth century records, called *rolls of arms*, were being compiled, because some of these have come down to us, either as originals or copies of lost originals. Some of these rolls contain the arms of nobles and knights present at a particular battle or tournament. Others are a general list of all the arms known to the compiler, or of knights in a particular locality.

Some of the rolls consisted of coloured sketches of shields with their owners' names written above them. Others were not illustrated, but consisted of descriptions of arms in words. Such verbal descriptions are called *blazons*. To blazon arms it was necessary to agree on terms for the various heraldic forms, and devise a phraseology by which designs could be described clearly and concisely. It seems probable that the heralds had a hand both in the compilation of the rolls of arms and in formulating the language of blazonry. This language was based on the French of the period, but in the course of time English words and phrases crept in with the result that the language of heraldry in this country is a mixture of French and English.

Blazons still follow the lines adopted in the thirteenth century. First the field is described—whether of one tincture, or party, varied, or semy with small charges; then the principal ordinary or charge occupying the central position, with any necessary descriptive words and its tincture; then the secondary charges with their tinctures. Unfortunately in later times the language of heraldry was unnecessarily complicated by roundabout phrases to avoid repeating tinctures, but in this book I have used a simple form of blazon which the reader who wishes to do so can easily master by comparing the descriptions of arms with the illustrations. Those who want fuller information about the language of heraldry may refer to such a book as *Boutell's Heraldry*.

As heraldry developed the heralds became more important. They ceased to be concerned mainly with tournaments, and became specialists in everything to do with chivalry, and were employed as messengers in war and peace. Not only kings and princes but also nobles and important knights had their own heralds, and it became the custom for a herald travelling on his master's business to wear a tabard, or loose tunic, embroidered with his lord's arms on the front, back and sleeves. A herald thus apparelled was the personal representative of the lord he served, and an affront to the herald was an affront to his master. In war heralds were non-combatants and could carry messages between enemies without fear of being attacked. The senior heralds were called *kings of heralds of arms*, shortened to *kings of arms*. These generally exercised heraldic jurisdiction in a particular district or province. In addition to the kings of arms and other heralds there were junior officers called *pursuivants of arms* who followed and assisted the heralds with a view to learning their duties and being promoted to the position of herald when they had become proficient. As more and more people began to use armorial bearings—not only men of the warrior class but also churchmen and merchants—it became necessary to make rules to prevent the infringement of arms and to restrict their use to those authorized to bear them, and the kings of arms, acting under the Earl Marshal, became the authorities through which the Sovereign exercised control over heraldry. In the fifteenth century they were required to compile records of all arms in use in their provinces, and empowered to grant arms to suitable persons who wanted them but had not inherited them from their ancestors. Thereafter arms could no longer be assumed at will, but could only be borne by those who had inherited them or had received a grant from the kings of arms. To this day the kings of arms, under the authority of the Earl Marshal (the Duke of Norfolk) continue to grant arms to suitable persons who apply to them, and also to corporate bodies.

33. Arms of branches of the Stafford family.

# 3. Heraldry and the Family

ALTHOUGH armorial bearings began simply as distinctive marks on shields and seals, they quickly acquired a significance and importance apart from their practical purpose. When a man adopted a personal device and consistently used it as his cognizance in war and his signature in peace, it soon became as much part of him as his name. Indeed, it might mean more to him than his name, because there might well be other men of the same name but nobody else bore exactly the same arms. As I have mentioned, arms were sometimes duplicated by accident, but the disputes to which this gave rise emphasized the principle that no two men should bear the same devices on their shields and seals, not only because this might lead to confusion between them but also because men regarded their arms as an intimate personal possession.

Of course, as arms were hereditary a son on growing to manhood would use his father's arms, but he did so with a *difference*—that is to say, he made some minor change or addition to the arms which would make them distinct from his father's while still preserving the essential similarity of their shields. In the case of the eldest son this difference was usually a *label*—a narrow bar with a number of pendants (generally three or five) laid horizontally across the shield. This is shown on the arms of John, eldest son of the first Earl of Westmoreland, in Fig. 34. (The Earl's first son by his second marriage also had a label, but it was differenced from his elder brother's as explained on page 41.) Occasionally a label is found not only on the shield but also on the crest. For example, in the crest of the Black Prince (Fig. 78) the lion wears a label in the form of a collar. The label is still the recognized mark of difference of the eldest son. When the father dies the eldest son removes the label from his shield and bears the undifferenced arms as head of the family.

Younger sons were in a different position from the first-born. None of them would succeed to their father's lordship or manor unless their elder brother died leaving no son. Consequently the differences they made in the arms, to distinguish them from their father's and from one another's, were permanent—that is to say they were not removed when the father died but continued to be borne by the younger sons and were in due course passed on to their descendants. In early heraldry these differences to denote younger sons took various forms. They might consist of a change in the tinctures of the shield, or the addition of a bendlet across it or a border round it, or the inclusion of one or more additional charges. In this way new shields of arms came into existence for the various branches of a family, each distinct from the other but containing as its principal feature the main charge in the original arms. Fig. 33 shows the arms of various branches of the Stafford family, all different but all incorporating the red chevron on a gold shield forming the original arms. In this case the additions made by the various branches were a black engrailed border, a blue chief, ermine quarter, a gold molet, three silver roundles, three black martlets, and three red martlets with three gold roundles on the chevron. The last shield is the result of the arms being differenced in two generations.

In three or four generations alterations and additions by younger sons and again by their younger sons could produce arms differing considerably from the original. This could scarcely be avoided in large families, each member of which wished to bear the original arms but with sufficient changes to make him clearly recognizable by his shield and surcoat when several members of the family were present at a battle or tournament. However, in the first half of the fifteenth century the shield ceased to be carried in war, and about the same time the surcoat went out of fashion. Heraldry continued to be used on seals, in pageantry and in the decoration of buildings and monuments, but it was no longer necessary for the differences made by younger members of a family to be so noticeable as they had to be when men relied on their arms for recognition in the field. Consequently it became the custom for younger sons to alter the arms as little as possible, and to add a single small charge to indicate their position in the family.

As an example of this, Fig. 34 shows the additions to their father's arms made by the sons of Ralph Nevill, first Earl of Westmoreland (1364–1425), who bore, Gules, a saltire argent.

John, the Earl's eldest son by his first marriage, differenced his father's arms with a blue label. He died before his father, and his son Ralph succeeded as second Earl and bore the undifferenced arms of his grandfather.

By his second marriage the first Earl had four sons. Richard, the first-born of this marriage but the Earl's second son, also bore his father's arms with a label, but to distinguish it from his step-brother's label, he made it of alternate white and blue squares (*compony* argent and azure). In Richard's case the label was a permanent addition to the arms, because the undifferenced arms were passed down with the earldom of Westmoreland to his elder brother's son.

The first Earl's younger sons, William, George and

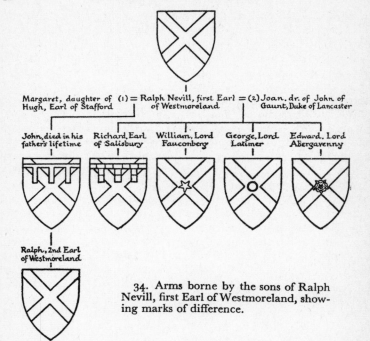

34. Arms borne by the sons of Ralph Nevill, first Earl of Westmoreland, showing marks of difference.

Edward, added to their father's arms a red molet, a black annulet and a red rose respectively, and these were permanent additions which were passed down to their descendants. Edward was the ancestor of the Marquess of Abergavenny whose arms are shown in Fig. 7.

At this time there was no definite rule as to the charge a younger son added to his arms to denote his position in the family. He might choose anything he pleased. Edward, Lord Abergavenny, probably chose a red rose because it was a badge of his mother's family. However, in the latter part of the fifteenth century the system was standardized. A label continued to be the recognized mark of the eldest son during his father's lifetime, while the permanent marks added by

35. Modern marks of difference for cadency.

the other sons were a crescent for the second son, a molet for the third, a martlet for the fourth, and so on, as shown in Fig. 35. These marks are still in use in England, but Scotland has a different system of denoting *cadency*. In theory these marks can themselves be charged with marks of cadency. Thus, a second son having added a crescent to his father's arms, his second son would place a crescent on the crescent, his third son a molet on the crescent, and so on. Actually this is quite impracticable, and although you may come across instances of it most people, if they use marks of cadency at all, are content with a single mark showing the particular branch of the family they belong to. It must be remembered that crescents, molets, martlets, annulets, fleurs-de-lis and so on are not only used as marks denoting younger sons. They are all common emblems in heraldry and are frequently found as charges in arms. You can usually tell when one of them appears as a mark of cadency because in this case it will be close to the top of the shield (or sometimes at the middle point) and drawn much smaller than the other charges.

A man's daughters might display his arms on seals or in personal decoration, but as they did not use them for the purpose of recognition they did not add differencing marks. It became the custom (which still prevails) for unmarried women to place their father's arms on a lozenge, or sometimes on a round or oval shape, but when a woman married her arms were placed on a shield with her husband's. Since women did not wear helms they did not (and still do not) use crests. This does not apply to a reigning queen, who bears the whole Royal Arms with shield, crest and supporters just as a king would do.

At an early date it became customary to indicate marriages heraldically by grouping the arms of husband and wife together on seals and in other ways. At first this was done by

36. De Valence.    De Valence dimidiated    De Chatillon.
                   with De Chatillon.

simply placing the arms side by side. Later they were combined on one shield. The earliest method of doing this was
by *dimidiation*—that is to say, the two coats were figuratively
cut down the middle and the dexter half of the husband's
arms was joined to the sinister half of the wife's. Fig. 36
shows the arms of Aymer de Valence, Earl of Pembroke
(*c.* 1280–1324) and of his wife Mary de Chatillon, daughter
of Guy, Count of St Pol, and the way they were combined
by dimidiation. The central shield is now the arms of Pembroke College, Cambridge, founded by the Countess. In
some cases this process of halving the arms made them unidentifiable (for example, half a chevron would appear to
be a bend) and accordingly dimidiation was replaced by
*impalement*. In this case the shield is divided by a vertical line
(or *party per pale*), the whole of the husband's arms being
placed in the dexter half and the whole of the wife's in the
sinister. Fig. 37 shows the arms of Nicholas Wadham (1532–
1609) and his wife Dorothy, daughter of Sir William Petre,
and how they were combined by impalement. They were the
founders of Wadham College, Oxford, which still uses the
shield with the impaled arms.

Impaled arms were borne only by the married pair and
were not passed down to their children. Usually children

37. Wadham.  Wadham impaling  Petre.
        Petre.

inherited only their father's arms. However, if their mother had no brothers to carry on her father's line the position was different. In this case she was her father's heiress (or co-heiress if she had a sister), and when he died his lordship would pass through her to her husband and their descendants. The arms went with the lordship, and the children of a man who married an heiress inherited the arms of both their parents and passed them down to their descendants. To show that the arms were permanently united a different method from impalement was adopted. The shield was *quartered*—that is, it was divided into four by intersecting vertical and horizontal lines—and the father's arms were placed in the first and fourth quarters and the mother's in the second and third. If the lordship derived from the mother was more important than that held by the father, the arms relating to it might be placed in the first and fourth quarters, the father's arms being relegated to the second and third.

Fig. 38 shows how the arms of Montagu (Argent, three lozenges joined fesswise gules) and Monthermer (Or, an eagle displayed vert) were quartered as a result of the marriage of Sir John Montagu with the heiress of Lord Monthermer. Sir John's elder brother was the second Earl of Salisbury, whose only son died in his lifetime. Sir John did not

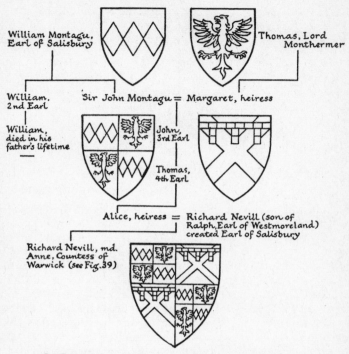

William Montagu,
Earl of Salisbury

Thomas, Lord
Monthermer

William,
2nd Earl

Sir John Montagu = Margaret, heiress

William,
died in his
father's lifetime

John,
3rd Earl

Thomas,
4th Earl

Alice, heiress = Richard Nevill (son of
Ralph, Earl of Westmoreland)
created Earl of Salisbury

Richard Nevill, md.
Anne, Countess of
Warwick (see Fig. 39)

38. Quartering of arms on marriage with heiresses.

live to succeed to the earldom, but it passed to his son and
grandson, who bore the arms, *Quarterly Montagu and Monthermer*. The fourth Earl's only daughter and heiress, Alice,
married Richard Nevill who (as shown in Fig. 34) bore,
*Gules, a saltire argent* differenced by a label compony argent
and azure. On his marriage Richard was created Earl of
Salisbury, and quartered his arms with the already quartered
arms of his wife. As the earldom came to him through his
wife, he placed her arms in the first and fourth quarters of
the shield and his own in the second and third quarters, producing the shield shown at the bottom of Fig. 38.

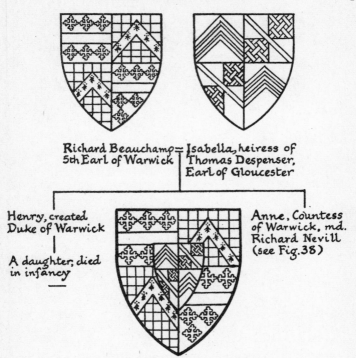

39. Arms of an heiress placed on an inescutcheon.

Fig. 39 shows the arms of Richard Beauchamp, 5th Earl of Warwick, and of Isabella, daughter and heiress of Thomas Despenser, Earl of Gloucester, and the way the arms were combined when they married. Each already had a quartered shield. Richard's contained the arms of Beauchamp (Gules, a fess between six cross-crosslets or) quartering those of the former Earls of Warwick (Checky or and azure, a chevron ermine). Isabella showed the Despensers' descent from the heiress of Gilbert de Clare, Earl of Gloucester, by quartering the arms of Clare (Or, three chevronels gules), and Despen-

40. Arms of Richard Nevill, Earl of Warwick and of Salisbury, 'the Kingmaker'.

ser (Quarterly argent and gules fretty gold, over all a bendlet sable). Isabella's father had been executed as a traitor and his earldom forfeited, and she carried to her husband the barony of Despenser but not the title of Gloucester. In this case her arms were placed on an escutcheon in the middle of her husband's shield. When Henry, Duke of Warwick (the only son of this marriage) and his only daughter died, his sister Anne became Countess of Warwick. She married Richard Nevill, whose arms are shown at the foot of Fig. 38, and he was created Earl of Warwick in 1449. At his father's death in 1460 Richard succeeded as Earl of Salisbury. His arms were combined with those of his wife in the manner shown in Fig. 40. The shield reflects the extent of his possessions and the concentration of power in his hands, through which he was able so greatly to influence the affairs of his time as to earn the name of 'Kingmaker'.

Complicated arms like these were not placed on the shield a man carried for defence in war. They belong to the period when the shield and surcoat had gone out of fashion except on occasions of pageantry. Although heraldry ceased to have any practical use in warfare it became increasingly important in other ways. Armorial bearings had become the symbol of the family—not only of the great ruling families like the Nevills, but also of the many families of lesser standing which were nevertheless conscious of their knightly status. Their arms stood for the ties of kinship between their various branches, the pride they felt in the achievements of their ancestors, and their hopes that future generations would carry on the tradition.

The possession of armorial bearings had become the sign of a certain position in society, and those rising in the social scale, such as prosperous merchants, wished to have arms for use on their seals and in other ways, though the day had passed when they could actually carry them on shields and surcoats. The kings of arms were empowered to grant arms and crests to people of suitable standing who had not inherited any from their ancestors. Consequently heraldry continued as a matter of dignity, just as knighthood and the orders of chivalry continued. In the latter part of the fifteenth century the kings of arms began the practice of visiting various parts of the country periodically to record arms in use, to stop people using them without a legal right, and to devise and grant new arms where necessary. Such visitations took place at intervals during the next two hundred years, and in conducting them the kings of arms, and the heralds assisting them, made records of the descent of many families. These records still exist at the College of Arms and are a valuable source of information in the sphere of genealogy.

One result of these visitations was to make not only the noble families but also those of no greater rank than knights and squires interested in their history and anxious to illustrate it in their armorial bearings. Figs. 38 and 39 have shown how in the fourteenth and fifteenth centuries men incorporated in their shields the arms of heiresses from whom they had derived some lordship or estate. In the sixteenth century this practice was carried farther. Men looked back over their pedigrees, and introduced into their shields the arms of any heiress an ancestor had married, even though she might have inherited from her father nothing but his surname and arms. In this way shields of arms became genealogical records. In many cases the four parts of a quartered shield would not accommodate the arms of all these heiresses, and it became necessary to divide the shield into six, eight, twelve, sixteen or more parts. When the number exceeded four the divisions of the shield were called *quarterings*. Rules (which still prevail) were laid down for the *marshalling* of arms—that is, the arrangement of two or more different coats of arms on one shield to denote descent from various families. The present practice is set out below.

When a man marries a woman who has brothers to carry on her father's family, and who therefore is not an heiress, he impales his arms with those of his wife in the manner already described and illustrated in Fig. 37. The wife also bears the impaled arms on a shield. Their children inherit only their father's arms.

When a man marries an heiress (or co-heiress) he places her father's arms in a small escutcheon on his own shield. This is called an *escutcheon of pretence* because it shows that the husband, on behalf of his wife, pretends (or claims) to represent her family in the absence of any male heir. Their children are in a different position. They are actually descended from and represent their mother's family. Accordingly they quarter the arms of their parents, placing their father's arms in the first and fourth quarters and their mother's in the second and third, and they pass these quartered arms on to their descendants.

In the imaginary pedigree shown in Fig. 41, John Pale married Mary Fess, an heiress, and placed her arms on an escutcheon of pretence on his own shield. Their son Henry bore *Quarterly Pale and Fess*. He married Jane Cross, also an heiress, and placed her arms in pretence on his own, and their son Richard placed the Cross arms in the third quarter of his shield. Richard married Ann Bend, also an heiress, and the process was repeated, the Bend arms being placed in the fourth quarter of the shield. And so it might go on, but of course next time a member of the family married an heiress his son would have to divide his shield into six quarterings, putting the heiress's arms in the fifth quartering and repeating the Pale arms in the sixth for the sake of balance.

If an heiress herself has a quartered shield (as a result of

John Pale = Mary, dr & hrs of A. Fess

Henry Pale = Jane, dr & hrs of B. Cross

Richard Pale = Ann., dr & hrs of C. Bend

James Pale

41. Modern method of quartering arms on marriage with heiresses.

the marriage of an ancestor with the heiress of some other
family), she passes the quarters on to her children. Fig. 42
gives actual instances of this. (Here I have omitted the shields
bearing the escutcheons of pretence, but you may assume that
Sir John Wrythe, William Wrythe and Sir Thomas Wrythe
each placed his wife's arms in pretence on his own shield.)
Januarius Dunstanville bore *Quarterly Dunstanville and Lushill*
because his grandfather had married the heiress of the
Lushill family. His daughter Barbara passed these arms on
to her son, William Wrythe, who accordingly bore *Quarterly,
1 and 4 Wrythe, 2 Dunstanville, 3 Lushill*. William's wife (also
an heiress) had a quartered shield, viz. *Quarterly, 1 and 4
Drayton, 2 Crowton, 3 Peckham*. Their son, Sir Thomas, added
these quarters to those he inherited from his father and bore
*Quarterly of six, 1 Wrythe, 2 Dunstanville, 3 Lushill, 4 Drayton,
5 Crowton, 6 Peckham*. Sir Thomas also married an heiress who
bore *Quarterly Cheyney and Lovetoft*, and his son added these
arms to the shield, which then consisted of eight quarterings,
described below.

This building up of shields of many quarterings was very
popular in the sixteenth and seventeenth centuries, and you
will find many examples on monuments in churches. However, heraldic taste has changed, and at the present time
most people possessing such elaborate shields actually display only two or three of the most important quarterings.

Quarterings in the bottom shield on the opposite page:

3. Argent, five lozenges joined palewise gules within a bordure
   azure charged with gold roundles—*Lushill*.
4. Per pale indented gules and azure, a lion rampant or—*Drayton*.
5. Argent, a chevron between three crows sable, on the chevron a
   gold crescent for difference—*Crowton*.
6. Sable, a chevron or between three cross-crosslets fitchy argent—
   *Peckham*.
7. Checky or an azure, a fess gules fretty argent—*Cheyney*.
8. Or, a lion rampant party per fess sable and gules—*Lovetoft*.

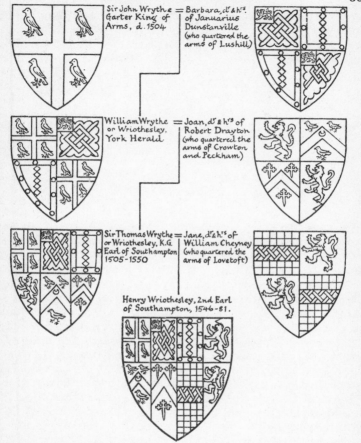

Sir John Wrythe Garter King of Arms, d. 1504 = Barbara, d⁵ & h⁵. of Januarius Dunstanville (who quartered the arms of Lushill)

William Wrythe or Wriothesley. York Herald = Joan, d⁵ & h⁵ of Robert Drayton (who quartered the arms of Crowton and Peckham)

Sir Thomas Wrythe or Wriothesley, K.G. Earl of Southampton 1505-1550 = Jane, d⁵ & h⁵ of William Cheyney (who quartered the arms of Lovetoft)

Henry Wriothesley, 2nd Earl of Southampton, 1546-81.

42. Table showing how the quarterings in the arms of Henry Wriothesley, second Earl of Southampton, were acquired. The quarterings are:

1. Azure, a cross between four falcons argent with gold bells—*Wrythe* or *Wriothesley*.

2. Argent, a fret gules within a bordure engrailed sable, on a canton gules a lion passant or—*Dunstanville*.

Peers     Baronets and     Esquires and
        Knights         Gentlemen

43. Types of Helm.

# 4. Signs of Rank and Office

WE have seen how a shield on which two or more coats of arms are marshalled may tell something about the families from which the owner is descended or with which he is connected by marriage. A complete achievement of arms often tells a great deal more than this. The type of helm bearing the crest shows whether the owner is a peer, a baronet or knight, or an esquire or gentleman. If he is a peer his shield is placed between supporters and the achievement includes his coronet, the type of coronet showing whether he is a duke, marquess, earl, viscount or baron. The arms of a baronet may be recognized by the baronet's badge on the shield or suspended below it. Knighthood or membership of one of the Orders of Chivalry is indicated by insignia surrounding the shield or placed beneath it. In addition to these signs of rank you may sometimes find in armorial bearings the symbols of some official position held by their owner.

## Helms

The types of helm denoting various ranks are:

For the Sovereign and Royal Princes: a gold barred helm, set full-face above the shield (see frontispiece).

For peers: a barred helm of silver decorated with gold, set sideways above the shield (Fig. 43).

For baronets and knights: a vizored helm of steel with the vizor raised, usually set full-face.

For esquires and gentlemen: a closed helm of steel, usually set sideways. This type of helm is also used by most corporations possessing crests.

It is customary for helms placed sideways above the shield to face towards the dexter side, and the crest must, of course, face the same way as the helm which bears it. The practice of placing an esquire's helm sideways and a knight's helm full-face is not always followed. If a knight having a lion passant as a crest placed it on a full-face helm, the lion would look out over the knight's right ear instead of facing the enemy. Accordingly in such cases the helm may be placed above the shield in the position best suited to the crest.

These different types of helm for various ranks were only introduced in the seventeenth century. In the heraldry of medieval and Tudor times there were no particular rules about helms, and if you look at the drawing of Sir Francis Drake's arms (Fig. 53) you will see they are shown with a closed sideways helm, while an open facing helm is shown in the achievement of Sir John Hawkins (Fig. 52).

## Peers' Coronets

In the achievement of a peer his coronet may be placed above the crest or shown resting on the top of the shield with the crested helm above it. The crimson cap with its gold tassel worn under the coronet may be included or not at will. The coronets appropriate to the various degrees in the peerage are shown in Fig. 44. These are:—

Royal Dukes: a coronet consisting (like the Royal Crown) of alternate crosses and fleurs-de-lis but without arches, and with the rim chased as jewelled—i.e. decorated with the shapes of jewels in relief but without any actual stones or colour.

E

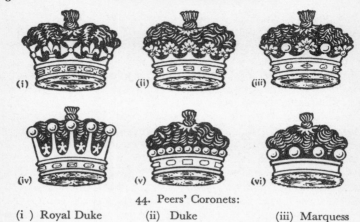

44. Peers' Coronets:

(i ) Royal Duke    (ii) Duke    (iii) Marquess
(iv) Earl    (v) Viscount    (vi) Baron

Dukes: a silver-gilt rim chased as jewelled set with eight strawberry-leaves (of which five are seen in drawings).

Marquesses: a similar rim set with four strawberry-leaves alternating with four silver balls.

Earls: a similar rim with eight points each topped by a silver ball.

Viscounts: a similar rim set with sixteen silver balls (of which nine are seen in drawings).

Barons: a plain silver-gilt rim set with six large silver balls (of which four are seen in drawings).

A peeress also places the appropriate coronet above her arms, and her shield (bearing her husband's arms marshalled with her own) between supporters, but she does not use a crest. A widowed peeress continues to use her married arms (with coronet and supporters) but places them on a lozenge.

The eldest son of a duke, marquess or earl is frequently called by one of his father's secondary titles; for example, the Duke of Bedford's eldest son is known as Marquess of Tavistock. This, however, is a courtesy title, and the person using it is not a peer. Consequently he is not entitled to a coronet

45. Insignia of Baronets.

or supporters in his achievement of arms. He only uses them when he succeeds to the peerage on the death of his father.

## Baronets' Badges

The hereditary Order of Baronets was founded in England in 1611 and extended to Ireland in 1619. A separate Order was established in Scotland in 1625. Holders of the older baronetcies are still known as Baronets of England, of Ireland, or of Scotland, but in the case of those created after the Union of England and Scotland in 1707 they are Baronets of Great Britain, while those made since the union of Great Britain and Ireland in 1801 are Baronets of the United Kingdom.

Baronets of England, of Ireland, of Great Britain and of the United Kingdom bear as an augmentation on their shields an escutcheon argent charged with a sinister hand gules (Figs. 45 (ii) and 63). The red hand is the badge of Ulster, which was adopted as the sign of a baronet because the earlier baronetcies were created to promote the plantation of Ulster. On ceremonial occasions baronets wear an oval badge consisting of the red hand on a shield with a crown above it within a border decorated with roses for Baronets of England, shamrock for Baronets of Ireland, roses and thistles for Baronets of Great Britain, and roses, thistles and shamrock for Baronets of the United Kingdom (Fig. 45 (i)). The badge is worn on an orange ribbon with a dark blue edge.

The Order of Baronets in Scotland was founded in connection with a scheme to colonize Nova Scotia. Originally these baronets were entitled to bear on a canton on their shields the arms of Nova Scotia—Azure, the saltire of St Andrew argent and over all an escutcheon of the Royal Arms of Scotland. They were also granted an oval badge consisting of these arms with the Royal Crown above them surrounded by the motto *Fax mentis honestae gloria* ('Glory is the torch of a noble mind') (Fig. 45 (iii)). It is now the practice for Baronets of Scotland to suspend this badge below their shields by an orange tawny ribbon.

Only the actual holder of a baronetcy is entitled to place the baronet's badge on or below his shield. His successors in the honour do so in their turn, but other members of the family bear the arms without these signs.

## Insignia of Knighthood

There are two main classes of Knighthood: Knights of one of the Orders of Chivalry, such as the Garter, the Thistle or the Bath, and those who do not belong to such an Order and are known as Knights Bachelor.

*The Most Noble Order of the Garter* was founded by Edward III in 1348. Its original insignia consisted of a blue Garter with a gold edge and buckle and bearing in letters of gold the inscription, *Honi soit qui mal y pense* ('Dishonoured be he who thinks evil of it'). The Garter was worn below the left knee. Soon after its foundation it became the custom for the Sovereign and Knights of the Order to place the Garter round their shields in representations of their arms, and this is still done (see frontispiece). Henry VII added to the insignia of the Order a collar which may also be placed round a knight's shield outside the Garter, though in these days most knights are content to display only the Garter. This collar, which is of gold enamelled in colour, consists of twenty-four red roses each within a blue Garter with its motto in gold and linked by gold knots. (In achievements of arms the collar may be

Military    **THE BATH**    Civil     **ST. MICHAEL AND ST. GEORGE**

**ROYAL VICTORIAN · BRITISH EMPIRE · KNIGHT BACHELOR.**

46. Insignia of Knighthood.

shown with fewer than twenty-four roses.) From the collar hangs the 'George'—a badge representing St George on horseback slaying the dragon, also enamelled in colour. Knights of the Garter also have other insignia and ceremonial garments, but we are concerned here only with those shown in conjunction with their armorial bearings.

Knights of other Orders of Chivalry founded in later centuries followed the practice of the Knights of the Garter in surrounding their shields with a coloured circle bearing the motto of their Order, but these circles are without the buckle and hanging tongue characteristic of the Garter. All these Orders also have distinctive collars, badges and ribbons. The circles and mottoes of the Orders are as follows. In each case the motto is in gold letters and the circle is edged with gold.

*The Most Ancient and Most Noble Order of the Thistle:* Green: *Nemo me impune lacessit* ('No one touches me with impunity').

*The Most Illustrious Order of St Patrick:* Sky-blue: *Quis separabit MDCCLXXXIII* ('Who shall separate?' 1783—the year of foundation).

*The Most Honourable Order of the Bath:* Red: *Tria juncta in uno* ('Three joined in one').

*The Most Distinguished Order of St Michael and St George:* Blue: *Auspicium melioris aevi* ('Token of a better age').

*The Royal Victorian Order:* Blue: *Victoria.*

*The Most Excellent Order of the British Empire:* Scarlet: *For God and the Empire.*

In addition to the circle, Knights of the Thistle and St Patrick may surround their shields with the collar of the Order. The collar of the Thistle consists of alternate sprigs of thistle and rue from which hangs the badge bearing the figure of St Andrew. That of St Patrick is composed of alternate harps and red and white roses, with a badge containing a red saltire surmounted by a shamrock charged with three crowns.

In the case of the other Orders only the Knights Grand Cross may place the collar round their arms. The other knights use only the circle with the badge of the Order hanging below it. The badges are illustrated in Fig. 46.

*Knights Bachelor* have the badge shown in Fig. 46, and this may be placed below their shields.

## Other Honours and Distinctions

In some of the Orders of Chivalry there are classes below that of Knight, members of which may show the insignia in their heraldic achievements.

Companions of the Bath and of St Michael and St George, and Commanders of the Royal Victorian Order and of the British Empire, may place the circle of their Order round their shields and hang its badge below. To tell whether a person displaying such insignia is a knight or a companion (or commander) you must look at the helm. A companion or commander will have an esquire's helm—unless, of course,

he is a peer or baronet in which case he will have the helm
and other signs of that rank.

Members of the Victorian Order, and Officers and Members of the Order of the British Empire, do not place the
circle of their Order round their shields, but they may hang
the badge below them. Their badges are similar in design to
those of knights but smaller.

There are certain other Orders of high standing which have
no class of knights but consist only of Members or Companions. These include the Order of Merit, the Order of
Companions of Honour, and the Distinguished Service
Order. Members may hang the badge of the Order below
their shields, and the same applies to other principal decora-
tions awarded by the Sovereign, such as the Victoria Cross.

An appointment to an Order of Chivalry is a personal
honour. The wife of a knight shares her husband's rank and
is addressed as 'Lady', but she is not a member of his Order,
unless she is appointed to it on her own merits. Consequently
the collar or circle of the Order conferred on a married man
is placed round a shield bearing his arms only, and not round
the combined arms of himself and his wife. If he wishes to include his wife's arms (impaled or in pretence), he must do so
on a separate shield alongside the one with the insignia
round it.

Similarly, when a married woman is a Dame or Commander of an Order of Chivalry it must be made clear in the
armorial bearings that the honour is hers and not her husband's. Here again two shields must be used side-by-side,
the dexter one bearing the husband's arms and the sinister
one the combined arms of husband and wife, and the insignia
must be placed round the sinister shield. In this case it is
correct to place the circle of the Order round the combined
arms, because a married woman can only bear her family
arms impaled with those of her husband or (if she is an heiress)
on an escutcheon within his shield. If both husband and wife
have been honoured each shield will have its appropriate
insignia.

## Insignia of Office

In the fourteenth century archbishops and bishops, regard-
ing themselves as married to their sees, began to impale the
arms of the sees with their personal arms in the same way
that husbands and wives combine their arms on one shield.
Later this practice was followed by some masters of colleges,
who impaled the college arms with their own, and in recent
times mayors of cities and boroughs, and chairmen of county
councils and other local government bodies, have been permitted to impale the arms of the council with their personal
arms. Official arms have been assigned to the Kings of Arms,
the Regius Professors at Cambridge and some others, and
these may also be impaled with the personal arms of the
holder of the office. In all cases the arms of the office are
placed in the dexter side of the shield. On retiring from the
office a man ceases to use the official arms. A married man
holding such an office does not impale his wife's arms on the
same shield that bears the official arms. The combined arms
of himself and his wife must be placed on a separate shield.

Official insignia may also be shown in connection with
armorial bearings. An archbishop or bishop places his mitre
above his shield and sometimes his cross, or crozier, diagonally behind it. The Earl Marshal of England (the Duke of
Norfolk) carries a gold baton tipped with black, and places
two such batons saltirewise behind his shield.

Kings of Arms have coronets, which they wear at the Coronation of a Sovereign. These are of silver-gilt and consist of
oak-leaves set on a circlet bearing the words *Miserere mei
Deus secundum magnam misericordiam tuam*, ('Have mercy upon
me, O God, after thy great goodness', from Psalm 51). A
King of Arms places his coronet above his shield, which is
surrounded by a collar composed of letters S which has
come down from the Lancastrian period. The Lord Chief
Justice of England, the Heralds and the Sergeants at Arms
also place this collar round their shields. Heralds and Pur-

47. Arms of John Fox, Bishop of Exeter.

48. Official Arms and Insignia of Garter King of Arms.

suivants of Arms have official badges which may be shown in conjunction with their armorial bearings.

Fig. 47 shows the arms of John Fox (*d.* 1528) when he was Bishop of Exeter, as they appear in Winchester Cathedral. On the dexter side are the arms of the See of Exeter (Gules, a sword erect, its blade silver and its hilt gold, surmounted by two gold keys saltirewise), and on the sinister side is a gold pelican on blue, the symbol of Corpus Christi which Fox used as a personal device. Above the shield is his mitre. The pelican also appears on the shield of Corpus Christi College, Oxford, which Fox (then Bishop of Winchester) founded in 1515.

Fig. 48 shows the official arms of Garter King of Arms surmounted by his coronet, encircled by the collar of SS and having two sceptres appropriate to his office crossed behind the shield. The arms are, Argent, a cross gules, on a chief azure a ducal coronet encircled by the garter between a lion passant gardant on the dexter side and a fleur-de-lis on the sinister side, all gold.

49. Douglas.      50. Pelham.      51. Howard with
                                   the augmentation
                                   for Flodden.

# 5. Some Historic Arms

EXCEPT for allusions to names, and emblems such as lions
and eagles typifying strength, fierceness and other warlike
qualities, early arms had little or no symbolic meaning—or
none that we can now trace. Very occasionally early shields
of arms are associated with some family tradition. For example, the Trevelyan arms of a white horse rising from water
in the lower part of the shield are said to commemorate that
the ancestor of the family lived in the old land of Lyonesse
beyond Land's End, and during the great storm in 1099
when Lyonesse was finally inundated by the sea he managed
to reach the Cornish coast on a swimming horse. Traditions
of this kind, however interesting, are not always true. It is
possible that the arms were originally adopted for some quite
different reason now forgotten, and that a romantic story
has been woven round them in later centuries.

The first trustworthy instance of arms commemorating an
historic event is provided by the shield of the Scottish family
of Douglas. The Douglas arms were originally, Argent, on a
chief azure three silver molets. When King Robert the Bruce
was dying he commanded that after his death his heart
should be taken from his body and carried to the Holy Land

for burial to fulfil a vow of pilgrimage he had been unable to undertake in his lifetime. The mission was entrusted to Sir James Douglas, who set forth in 1330, and as a sign of the duty on which he was engaged he displayed a red heart on his shield (Fig. 49). However, he did not reach Palestine, being killed in a battle against the Moors in Spain, and Bruce's heart was brought back to Scotland and buried at Melrose. Sir James Douglas's descendants continued to bear the heart in their arms, and eventually a Royal Crown was placed above it.

From the fourteenth century onwards additions were occasionally made to a man's arms to commemorate some outstanding service or exploit. These additions are called 'augmentations of honour'. An early example consists of two buckles with broken thongs, representing part of the sword belt of King John of France, granted to Sir John Pelham who was concerned in the King's capture at the Battle of Poitiers in 1356. These two buckles, silver on red, are quartered with the arms of Pelham (Azure, three pelicans argent) by Sir John's descendants, the Earls of Chichester and Yarborough (Fig. 50). The buckle is also used as a badge by the Pelham family, and may be seen carved on the font in Burwash church and elsewhere in Sussex.

One of the most notable augmentations was that granted to Thomas Howard, Earl of Surrey, for his victory over the Scots at the battle of Flodden in 1513. To his arms, Gules, a bend between six cross-crosslets fitchy argent, was added (on the bend) an escutcheon of the Royal Arms of Scotland but having the lion cut in half and pierced through the mouth by an arrow. This referred to the fact that King James IV of Scotland was slain in the battle, and his body was found pierced by arrows. This augmentation is still used by the Duke of Norfolk and other members of the Howard family (Fig. 51). Lord Wharton, who as captain of Carlisle inflicted a severe defeat on a Scottish army at Solway Moss in 1542, also received an augmentation. His original arms were, Sable, a maunch (lady's sleeve) argent. To these was added a gold

52. Sir John Hawkins.           53.  Sir Francis Drake.

border charged with eight pairs of lions' paws, torn off and
coloured gules, symbolizing the maiming of the Scottish lion.

The armorial bearings of two great seamen of the sixteenth
century are of historic interest. In 1565 John Hawkins
(knighted in 1588) was granted arms celebrating his voyages
to Africa and America. The arms were, Sable, on a base
wavy argent and azure a lion passant or and in chief three
golden roundles, denoting the English lion crossing the seas
and bringing back treasure of gold. Three years later on an
expedition to the West Indies Hawkins defeated a Spanish
captain and seized his ensign, which was gold with a scallop
between two palmers' staves sable. Accordingly in 1569 he
was granted this ensign as a canton of augmentation to his
arms. His crest was a bound and captive Moor (Fig. 52).

Sir Francis Drake's voyage round the world is recorded in
the armorial bearings granted to him in 1581. The arms are,

Sable, a fess wavy argent between two silver estoiles, representing his course on the waters and the stars by which he steered. The crest is a terrestrial globe surmounted by a ship under sail proper with gold hawsers whereby the vessel is drawn round the globe by a hand appearing out of clouds also proper, and in the ship a dragon gules, its wings spread, looking towards the hand (Fig. 53). The hand is that of God, whose aid is acknowledged by the motto, *Auxilio Divino* ('By divine assistance'). The dragon (or 'fire-drake') is a play on the name of Drake. This is an instance of the elaborate crests which were sometimes granted in the days when heraldry was no longer actually worn. One cannot imagine a knight going into action with such a towering structure on his helm.

A later shield representing voyages of discovery is that granted in 1785 to the descendants of Captain James Cook to commemorate his explorations. This is azure with a gold estoile in the upper part of the shield and another in the point, and between the estoiles a terrestrial sphere showing the Pacific Ocean bounded on one side by America and on the other by Asia and New Holland( i.e. Australia), with the track of Captain Cook's voyages marked in red lines. A still later example of exploration recorded in heraldry is found in the arms granted to the family of Captain John Hanning Speke, discoverer of the source of the Nile. The original arms were, Argent, two bars azure and over all a two-headed eagle displayed gules. In 1867, after Speke's death, his work was commemorated by the grant to his father of an addition to the shield consisting of a chief azure and thereon a representation of flowing water proper and above it the word 'Nile' in gold letters. A crest of augmentation consisting of a crocodile was also granted, to be borne alongside the original crest of the family, which was a porcupine. Supporters consisting of a crocodile and a hippopotamus were also added to the achievement. This is an unusual instance of the grant of supporters to an untitled person, but probably had Captain Speke lived longer he would have received some honour

54. Newman.     55. Carlos.     56. Lane.

entitling him to bear supporters. The augmentation of arms and crest were intended to pass down in the usual way to the descendants, but the supporters were granted to Captain Speke's father only for his lifetime, and were no doubt meant to be used on a memorial to the explorer.

During the years that Charles II spent in exile, and after his restoration to the throne in 1660, heraldic honours were accorded to a number of people who had given signal support to the Royalist cause. The most interesting of these are arms or augmentations granted to those who assisted Charles's escape after the Battle of Worcester. Colonel Richard Newman, whose conduct at Worcester enabled the Prince to escape through the City gate, was granted an escutcheon gules charged with a gold crowned portcullis as an addition to his arms, which were, Quarterly sable and argent, in the first and fourth quarters three silver molets (Fig. 54). Colonel William Carlos, who was the Prince's companion when he hid in the oak at Boscobel, was granted as arms a gold shield bearing an oak-tree proper, and over all a fess gules charged with three Royal Crowns (of England, Scotland and Ireland) also proper (Fig. 55), and as crest a crossed sword and sceptre within a wreath of oak. To commemorate the help rendered by Mistress Jane Lane, who rode from Bentley in Staffordshire to the Dorset border with Prince Charles disguised as her servant, her brother was granted a canton gules charged with the three gold lions of England as an addition to his arms, which were, Per fess or and azure, a chevron gules between three molets countercharged (Fig. 56). He was also granted as a crest a demi-horse of strawberry roan colour supporting the Royal Crown of gold—the horse on which the Prince had ridden with Mistress Jane on a pillion—together with the motto, *Garde le Roy*. This, together with the shield, may be seen on the inn-sign of The Lane Arms at Bentley (Fig. 150). During his wanderings the Prince was sheltered for two nights at Moseley Hall by Thomas Whitgreave, whose great-great-grandson received as a commemorative addition to his arms a red rose among gold rays within a wreath of oak proper.

Francis Mansell of Guildford, a merchant who provided the ship in which Charles was at last able to leave the country, was granted as arms, Or, three maunches sable and on a chief gules a gold lion of England, and as crest a black ship with one mast, its sail white, flying the cross of St George at masthead, bow and poop, and charged on the stern with three Royal Crowns proper.

Sir John Keith, Earl of Kintore, who saved the regalia of Scotland from falling into the hands of the Parliamentary forces, was granted as an addition to his arms (Argent, on a chief gules three pallets or) an escutcheon gules charged with a Royal Crown, sceptre and sword surrounded by eight thistles, all gold. The preservation of the regalia is also referred to in the arms of Kincardineshire (Fig. 120).

Among those who received augmentations to their arms at the Restoration was the first Sir Winston Churchill. To his family arms—Sable, a lion rampant argent—was added a canton argent charged with the red cross of St George. This appeared in the first and fourth quarters of the arms of his descendant, the late Sir Winston Churchill, K.G. The first Sir Winston's famous son, John Churchill, Duke of Marlborough, bore these arms with a number of quarterings. Marlborough left no son, and the dukedom passed through his daughter to Charles Spencer, Earl of Sunderland. The Spencer arms—Quarterly argent and gules fretty or, over all

57. The Duke of Marlborough.  58. Lord Heathfield.  59. Sir William Green.

a bend sable charged with three scallop-shells argent—were then quartered with those of Churchill. To commemorate the first Duke's victories his descendants received as a further augmentation an escutcheon argent bearing the red cross of St George and thereon another escutcheon charged with the arms of France—Azure, three gold fleurs-de-lis. This also appears in the shield of the present Duke of Marlborough and the late Sir Winston Churchill, K.G. (Fig. 57).

Augmentations were granted to a number of distinguished soldiers and sailors during the eighteenth and nineteenth centuries. Sir Augustus Eliott, Lord Heathfield, the defender of Gibraltar during the siege of 1779–83, bore, Gules, on a gold bend a baton azure. To this was added a chief of the arms of Gibraltar: Azure, between two pillars a castle argent with a gold key pendant from the gate and below it the words *Plus Ultra* (Fig. 58). Sir William Green, a military engineer who was responsible for the fortifications during the siege, was granted: Parted chevronwise vert and argent, in chief two silver castles and in base another castle surrounded by a fortification proper, over all a chevron or charged with three roundles gules. The red roundles represented red-hot cannonballs for which Green constructed kilns (Fig. 59).

Sir Horatio Nelson was granted as arms in 1797, Gold, a cross flory sable, a bend gules surmounted by a bend engrailed or and thereon three bombs with flames bursting

60. Sir Horatio
Nelson.

Viscount Nelson.

Earl Nelson.

from them proper; the cross being from the arms of the
family from which he was traditionally descended. After the
battle of the Nile he was created Baron (later Viscount)
Nelson of the Nile, and received as an augmentation to his
arms, a chief wavy argent, thereon waves of the sea with a
palm tree rising from them between a disabled ship and a
battery in ruins all in proper colours. Nelson's brother received the earldom which would have been conferred upon
Horatio but for his death at Trafalgar, and at the same time
the arms were further augmented by the addition of a fess
wavy azure charged with the word 'Trafalgar' in letters of
gold (Fig. 60). This is an instance of heraldic honours being
carried to the extent of defeating the original purpose of
heraldry, because the addition of the fess left little to be seen
of the cross which was the original charge in the Nelson arms.
The present Earl Nelson does not use the second augmentation.

Lord Collingwood, who was second in command at Trafalgar, bore, Argent, a chevron between three stags' heads
sable, and received as an augmentation a chief wavy gules
and thereon a gold lion of England with a gold naval
coronet on its head and above it the word 'Trafalgar' in gold
letters.

The arms of the Arthur Wellesley, Duke of Wellington,
were quarterly Wellesley (Gules, a cross argent between in

F

61. The Duke of          62. Earl          63. Sir Cecil
    Wellington.          Kitchener.           Chubb.

each quarter five silver roundles) and Colley (Or, a lion
rampant gules). In 1814 he was granted as an augmentation
the Union Badge of the United Kingdom—that is, the crosses
of St George, St Andrew and St Patrick combined as in the
Union flag but displayed upon a shield (Fig. 61).

Horatio Herbert, Earl Kitchener, received two augmentations. His original arms were, Gules, a chevron argent surmounted by a chevron azure between three bustards proper,
in the centre chief point a golden roundle. To this was added
in 1900, in commemoration of the recapture of Khartoum, a
gold pile charged with the Union Flag and the Egyptian
Flag saltirewise, their staves encircled by a mural crown
gules inscribed with the name Khartoum in gold. For the
South African campaign Lord Kitchener received as a
further addition a chief argent, thereon a pale gules charged
with a lion of England or, between to the dexter an eagle
sable (for the Transvaal) and to the sinister an orange tree
bearing fruit and growing from a mound all in proper
colours (for the Orange Free State) (Fig. 62). These arms
may be seen on a banner above his tomb in St Paul's
Cathedral.

Admiral Lord Fisher, who was an advocate of the battleship of the 'Dreadnought' type, was granted as arms, Argent,
in chief two demi-lions rampant gules and in base the stern

of an ancient battleship showing three lanterns proper, with the motto, 'Fear God and Dread Nought'.

The achievements not only of war but also of peace are commemorated in heraldry. For example, Robert Stevenson (grandfather of Robert Louis Stevenson), builder of lighthouses on the Scottish coast, was granted, Argent, on a chevron between three fleurs-de-lis azure three silver molets, with a chief silver and thereon rising from the sea and rocks the Bell Rock Lighthouse with a temporary lighthouse, men at work, and ships in the offing, all proper. This lighthouse, which was Stevenson's most notable work, was finished in 1812.

The arms granted to Sir Humphry Davy, inventor of the miner's safety lamp in 1815, were, Sable, a chevron engrailed gold ermined sable between in chief two gold annulets and in base a flame encompassed by a chain proper issuing from a gold oak-wreath.

The triumphs of astronomical science are represented in the arms granted to Sir William Herschel, discoverer of the planet Uranus in 1781: Argent, on a mount vert a representation of Herschel's forty-foot reflecting telescope with its apparatus proper, and on a chief azure the astronomical symbol of Uranus amid gold rays. This (like the arms of Nelson and Stevenson) is an instance of a bad period of heraldry when detailed pictorial scenes were introduced into shields instead of symbolic forms appropriate to heraldic art. By contrast, the arms granted to Sir Cecil Chubb, Bt., commemorating his presentation of Stonehenge to the nation in 1918, show how effectively simple heraldic forms may be used to convey a meaning. The arms are: Per fess azure and vert, two pales surmounted by a chief cut off at the ends argent (Fig. 63). Visualize this in colour, and you will see that it represents two of the upright stones of Stonehenge with a third stone lying on them, against a background of blue sky and green hillside. In the corner of the shield is the red hand on a white escutcheon denoting the arms of a baronet.

64. The Royal Crest of England, in Henry V's chantry, Westminster Abbey.

# 6. Royal Heraldry of Great Britain

THE Royal Arms of the United Kingdom are widely used and should be familiar to us all. We have only to look at a half-crown piece to see the quartered shield bearing the arms of England, Scotland and Ireland with the Crown above it, while this shield, encircled by the Garter, supported by the lion and unicorn and accompanied by the motto, *Dieu et mon droit*, appears on post offices and some other public buildings, on many government publications, and on shops and offices of firms which hold Royal Warrants. The Royal Arms have a long and interesting story which is closely connected with our national history, and they underwent many changes before they reached their present form when Queen Victoria came to the throne in 1837 (see frontispiece).

The Royal Arms are *Arms of Dominion* relating to Great Britain and Northern Ireland. They represent the realms over which the Sovereign reigns (or in the past has claimed to reign), and not the families from which the monarch of the day is descended. Accordingly in the present arms there is no quarter for the House of Saxe-Coburg and Gotha from which the Queen is descended in the male line through the Prince Consort of Queen Victoria. Similarly the Stuart Kings did not quarter the arms of the family of Stuart, nor the Tudor Sovereigns those of Tudor. Consequently the arms have not

74

necessarily changed when the Crown has passed from one family to another, but only when this has resulted in some change in the realms over which the Sovereign reigns. The royal shield remained the same from the time of Henry IV to that of Elizabeth I though during that period the crown passed from Lancaster to York and from York to Tudor. However, when James VI of Scotland came to the English throne the Royal Arms were altered to reflect the fact that he was King of both realms, and there were further changes in Hanoverian times.

In Plantagenet and Tudor times the family from which the Sovereign came was frequently indicated by the supporters of the royal shield and also by badges accompanying it, and although the shield remained unchanged from 1405 to 1603 the other parts of the achievement varied from reign to reign, and often enable us to tell which particular Sovereign the arms represent. In this chapter the development of the Royal Arms is traced under the headings of the various houses which have occupied the throne and the descent of the Crown is illustrated by tables.

Planta genista.     White Hart.     Sunburst.     Ostrich Feather.
65. Some Plantagenet badges.

## The House of Plantagenet

The House of Plantagenet is so called from its male ancestor, Geoffrey, Count of Anjou, who married Matilda (or Maud), the daughter of Henry I. He was nicknamed 'Plantagenet' because it was his custom to wear a sprig of *planta genista*, or broom plant, and this became a badge of his descendants (Fig. 65). As we have seen in Chapter I, he was given by his father-in-law, Henry I, a blue shield bearing a number of gold lions (Fig. 3). This is one of several reasons we have for believing that a lion was a royal badge in the time of Henry I. It is believed that his grandson Henry II bore two gold lions on red as arms, but there is no direct evidence of this. Both Henry II's sons bore lions on their shields. Richard I, the 'Lion-heart', had one lion rampant on his shield in his first Great Seal, and there is reason to believe that he sometimes used as a device two lions rampant combatant—that is, facing one another as though fighting. John, before he came to the throne, bore two lions passant. The first appearance of the three lions passant gardant was on the second Great Seal of Richard I which was made in 1195 (Fig. 4), and these, gold upon a red field, still occupy the first and fourth quarters of the royal shield. On this seal Richard was shown with a lion painted on the fan-shaped plate on the top of his helm, and this was the forerunner of the Royal Crest. Gules, three gold lions passant gardant, continued to be the Royal Arms of England until 1340 (see Table I).

In that year Edward III, whose mother was Isabella, daughter of Philip IV of France, began to use a quartered shield with the arms of France in the first and fourth quarters and those of England in the second and third. At this time the arms of France were, Azure semy of gold fleurs-de-lis (Fig. 27), which are known as *France Ancient*. Edward therefore bore *Quarterly France Ancient and England*, which may be seen on his tomb at Westminster, from which the shield at the foot of Table I is drawn. At the same time Edward put forward a claim to the French throne, so that the arms continued to be Arms of Dominion though the French quarters represented a claim to and not actual possession of that realm.

Edward III's crest was a gold-crowned lion standing on a red chapeau turned up with ermine, the mantling being also red lined with ermine. When the crest was actually worn on a

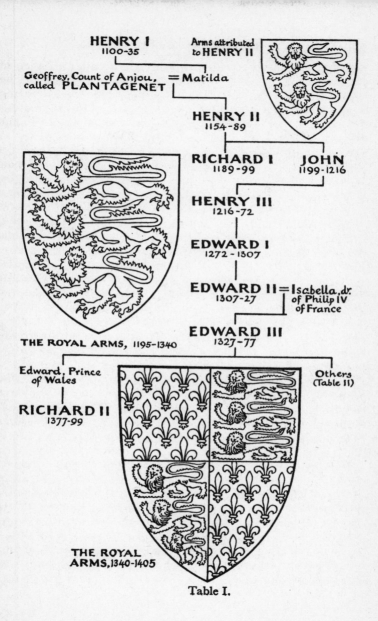

**HENRY I**
1100-35

Arms attributed to HENRY II

Geoffrey, Count of Anjou, called **PLANTAGENET** = Matilda

**HENRY II**
1154-89

**RICHARD I**    **JOHN**
1189-99      1199-1216

**HENRY III**
1216-72

**EDWARD I**
1272-1307

**EDWARD II** = Isabella, dr. of Philip IV of France
1307-27

**EDWARD III**
1327-77

**THE ROYAL ARMS, 1195-1340**

Edward, Prince of Wales

Others
(Table II)

**RICHARD II**
1377-99

**THE ROYAL ARMS, 1340-1405**

Table I.

helm the lion looked straight in front of it, as was only natural since it would scarcely turn its face away from the enemy against which it was advancing. It appears in this way in the stone carving of the Royal Crest in Henry V's chantry at Westminster Abbey (Fig. 64). However, on seals and paintings of the arms the lion was shown with its head turned so as to face the viewer, so that it was gardant like the ones in the shield; the crest continued in this form until the reign of Henry VIII. In some early representations of the crest, such as Fig. 64, the lion is uncrowned, but later it always had a crown on its head.

Edward III also had a number of badges, including a griffin, a bull, an eagle, a falcon, a boar, and a greyhound. Some of these were used by his sons and their descendants both as badges and also as supporters when these heraldic ornaments were introduced in the fifteenth century. The bull became the badge of his third son, Lionel, Duke of Clarence, and was passed down to become a supporter of Edward IV. The fourth son, John of Gaunt, used the eagle as a badge, and some of his descendants made it a supporter of their arms. The falcon was taken by the fifth son, Edmund Langley, Duke of York, and became associated with that dukedom. The greyhound became a Lancastrian badge, was granted to the first Tudor Earl of Richmond, and eventually became a badge and supporter of the Tudor sovereigns. Other badges of Edward III, also used by some of his descendants, included rays of the sun bursting through clouds, and an ostrich feather (Fig. 65).

Richard II used as a badge a white hart with a gold coronet about its neck and a gold chain attached—perhaps a 'rich hart' in allusion to his name (Fig. 65). In later times this was regarded as a supporter, and in King's College Chapel, Cambridge (and elsewhere) his arms may be seen held up by two harts. Another badge extensively used by Richard was the sun (to which Shakespeare frequently refers in the play *Richard II*), and his standard showed the hart accompanied by several suns. He sometimes impaled the

Royal Arms with those attributed to Edward the Confessor, who was at that time regarded as a national saint.

The Houses of Lancaster and York were branches of the Plantagenet line descended from different sons of Edward III, as shown in Table II. When Richard II was deposed his cousin Henry, Duke of Lancaster, son of John of Gaunt, took possession of the throne and ruled as Henry IV. In so doing he and those who supported him passed over his cousin, Roger Mortimer, Earl of March, who was the rightful heir to Richard II as a descendant of the next senior line to that from Edward, Prince of Wales. Roger did not press his claim, but his grandson, Richard, Duke of York, claimed the throne in the reign of Henry VI on the grounds that he was descended from Edward III by a line senior to that of Lancaster. The result was the dynastic struggle between two branches of the Royal House which is called the 'Wars of the Roses' from the fact that a red rose was a badge of Lancaster and a white rose that of York.

66. Antelope, Beacon and Swan:
Lancastrian badges in Westminster Abbey.

## The House of Lancaster

The Royal Arms continued to be *Quarterly France Ancient and England* until 1405. Meanwhile the French King had reduced the number of fleurs-de-lis in his shield to three, producing the arms of *France Modern*. Henry IV followed his example and from 1405 bore *Quarterly France Modern and England*, illustrated in Table II.

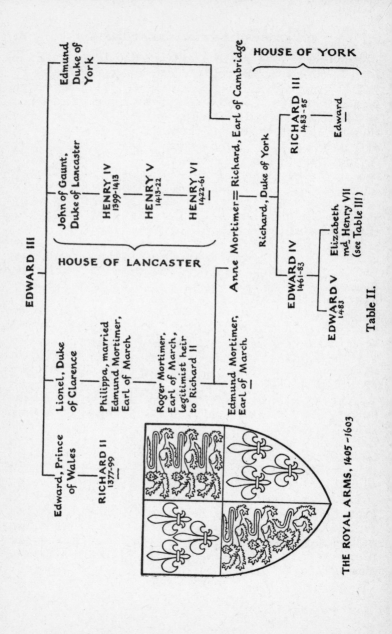

EDWARD III

Edward, Prince of Wales

RICHARD II
1377-99

Lionel, Duke of Clarence

Philippa, married Edmund Mortimer, Earl of March

Roger Mortimer, Earl of March, legitimist heir to Richard II

Edmund Mortimer, Earl of March

Anne Mortimer = Richard, Earl of Cambridge

John of Gaunt, Duke of Lancaster

HENRY IV
1399-1413

HENRY V
1413-22

HENRY VI
1422-61

HOUSE OF LANCASTER

Edmund Duke of York

HOUSE OF YORK

Richard, Duke of York

EDWARD IV
1461-83

RICHARD III
1483-85

EDWARD V
1483

Elizabeth md Henry VII
(see Table III)

Edward

THE ROYAL ARMS, 1405-1603

Table II.

Supporters of the Royal Arms were first actually used in the reign of Henry VI, but they were assigned to Henry IV and Henry V in some representations of their arms set up commemoratively after their reigns. The following are found as supporters of the arms of the Lancastrian kings (the dexter supporter being the first mentioned):

A gold lion and a white antelope—(attributed to) Henry IV and Henry V; used by Henry VI.

A white antelope and a white swan—(attributed to) Henry IV.

A gold lion and a gold panther spotted with various colours —Henry VI.

Two white antelopes—Henry VI.

The antelope and the swan were derived from badges of the family of Bohun, Henry IV's wife being Mary Bohun, daughter and co-heiress of Humphrey, Earl of Hereford. The panther was a Lancastrian device. These were also used separately as badges together with a number of others including the red rose of Lancaster (sometimes placed within rays of the sun), a cresset (or beacon) and a greyhound (from Edward III). The antelope, cresset and swan, as they appear in the carvings of Henry V's Chantry at Westminster Abbey, are illustrated in Fig. 66.

Closely associated with the House of Lancaster was the family of Beaufort, which was also descended from John of Gaunt, as shown in Table III. John Beaufort, who became Earl of Somerset, was born before the marriage of John of Gaunt to Catharine Swinford, and was therefore of illegitimate birth, though he was subsequently legitimated by Act of Parliament. The badge of the Beauforts was a portcullis (which later became a badge of the Tudor Sovereigns), and John, Duke of Somerset, used as supporters a gold eagle (from John of Gaunt) and a silver yale with gold spots which was probably a variant of the Lancastrian antelope. His daughter Margaret had two yales as supporters of her arms, as may be seen in Fig. 98.

67. Falcon and Fetter-
    lock of York.

68. White Rose en
    soleil of York,
    and White Lion of
    March.

69. Crowned
    Hawthorn
    of Henry
    VII.

## The House of York

The three Yorkist kings (see Table II) bore the Royal
Arms, *Quarterly France Modern and England,* with the following
supporters:

A gold lion and a black bull—Edward IV.
A black bull and a white lion—Edward IV.
Two white lions—Edward IV.
A white lion and a white hart—Edward IV and Edward V.
A gold lion and a white boar—Richard III.
Two white boars—Richard III.

The supporters of the Yorkist kings indicate their title to
the throne by descent from Lionel, Duke of Clarence,
through Edmund Mortimer, Earl of March. The black bull
was the badge of Clarence and the white lion that of March.
Edward IV used the white hart to show that he represented
the true line of succession from Richard II. From the Dukes
of York he had the badge of a silver falcon within a gold
fetterlock, and when he attained the throne the fetterlock
was shown a little open as though to indicate that the falcon
was no longer locked away from the throne but was free to
soar (Fig. 67). The boar used by Richard III as a badge and

supporter was probably derived from Edward III. Historically the most famous Yorkist badge is the white rose which was opposed to the red rose of Lancaster in the Wars of the Roses. The House of York also used Richard II's sun badge, and combined this with their rose to produce a white rose *en soleil*. This together with fleurs-de-lis, and the white lion of March amid suns, is shown in Fig. 68, drawn from a book of badges at the College of Arms.

70. Tudor Rose and Portcullis.

## The House of Tudor

Henry Tudor, Earl of Richmond, attained the throne by the defeat and death of Richard III at the battle of Bosworth. Henry's claim to the throne by descent from John of Gaunt (see Table III) was weakened by the illegitimate origin of the family of Beaufort, but he reinforced his position by marrying Elizabeth, daughter of Edward IV and heiress of the Yorkist line. This union of the two branches of the Plantagenets was signified by uniting the red rose of Lancaster and the white rose of York so as to produce the Tudor rose—a double rose usually consisting of red outer petals with a white centre but sometimes having the colours reversed. At Westminster Abbey, Windsor and elsewhere the Tudor rose

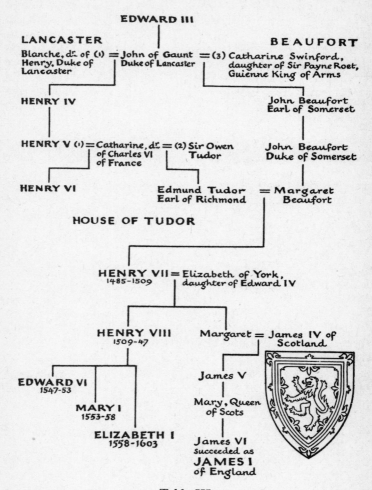

**EDWARD III**

**LANCASTER**

Blanche, dr. of (1) = John of Gaunt = (3) Catharine Swinford,
Henry, Duke of        Duke of Lancaster        daughter of Sir Payne Roet,
Lancaster                                        Guienne King of Arms

**BEAUFORT**

**HENRY IV**

John Beaufort
Earl of Somerset

**HENRY V** (1) = Catharine, dr. = (2) Sir Owen
                of Charles VI        Tudor
                of France

John Beaufort
Duke of Somerset

**HENRY VI**

Edmund Tudor           = Margaret
Earl of Richmond          Beaufort

**HOUSE OF TUDOR**

**HENRY VII** = Elizabeth of York,
1485–1509      daughter of Edward IV

**HENRY VIII**          Margaret = James IV of
1509–47                              Scotland

**EDWARD VI**          James V
1547–53

**MARY I**              Mary, Queen
1553–58                  of Scots

**ELIZABETH I**         James VI
1558–1603               succeeded as
                        **JAMES I**
                        of England

Table III.

is frequently seen with a crown above it, and often in close proximity to a crowned portcullis denoting the descent of the Tudor Sovereigns from the Beauforts (Fig. 70). They also used as badges, and as supporters of the Royal Arms, a red dragon alluding to Sir Owen Tudor's supposed descent from Cadwalader, the last native ruler of Britain, and a white greyhound associated with the earldom of Richmond but originally a Lancastrian emblem derived from Edward III. Another badge of Henry VII was a crowned hawthorn (Fig. 69) referring to the fact that after the battle of Bosworth Richard III's crown was found under a hawthorn and was placed on Henry's head. Queen Mary I derived from her mother, Catherine of Aragon, the badge of a pomegranate, which was sometimes shown joined to a Tudor rose. Queen Elizabeth I also used the badge of her mother, Anne Boleyn, a crowned falcon holding a sceptre, and she introduced into the royal badges a crowned harp to represent Ireland.

Throughout the Tudor period the Royal Arms continued to be *Quarterly France Modern and England*. Henry VIII introduced a change in the Royal Crest, making the lion gardant stand on the arches of a Royal Crown instead of on a chapeau. The mantling continued to be red lined with ermine until the reign of Elizabeth I, who made it gold lined with ermine. Since that time there has been no further change in the crest and mantling.

The supporters used by the Sovereigns of the House of Tudor were:

Two white greyhounds—Henry VII.

A red dragon and a white greyhound—Henry VII and Henry VIII.

A gold lion and a red dragon—Henry VII, Henry VIII, Edward VI and Mary I.

A red dragon and a black bull—Henry VIII. The bull denoted his descent through his mother from Edward IV and thence via Clarence from Edward III.

A red dragon and a white cock—Henry VIII. The cock (*gallus*) is thought to have been a play on the name of Wales (*Galles*).

A gold lion and a white greyhound—Mary I, Elizabeth I.

An eagle and a lion—Mary I on her marriage with Philip II of Spain.

A gold lion and a gold dragon—Elizabeth I.

### The House of Stuart

The descent of James VI of Scotland from Henry VII of England, by which he came to the English throne as James I, is shown in Table III. At his accession the Royal Arms of Scotland were brought into the shield and at the same time arms were introduced to represent Ireland. The Scottish arms were: Or, a lion rampant gules within a double tressure flory counter-flory gules—i.e. a double border set with fleurs-de-lis, their heads alternately outwards and inwards. The arms of Ireland were: Azure, a golden harp with silver strings. (The harp is found in different forms. It is sometimes decorated with a lion's head and sometimes with the head and wings of an angel. These are variations in artistic treatment, and have no heraldic significance.) From 1603 to 1688 the Royal Arms used in England were: *Quarterly*: 1 and 4, *France Modern and England quarterly; 2, Scotland; 3, Ireland.* In Scotland the arms were differently arranged. So far as the Scots were concerned, their King had acceded to another throne but he was still first and foremost King of Scotland. Accordingly they placed the Scottish arms in the principal quarters of the shield—namely the first and fourth —relegating the quartered arms of France and England to the second quarter and leaving those of Ireland in the third. Both forms of the Royal Arms are illustrated in Table IV.

In England the Royal Crest continued to be the gold crowned lion statant gardant on the Royal Crown, but in Scotland the Scottish Royal Crest was used, namely a red

## HOUSE OF STUART

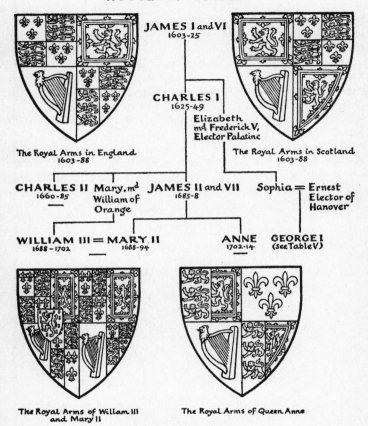

JAMES I and VI
1603-25

CHARLES I
1625-49

Elizabeth
m⁴ Frederick V,
Elector Palatine

The Royal Arms in England
1603-88

The Royal Arms in Scotland
1603-88

CHARLES II    Mary, m⁴    JAMES II and VII    Sophia = Ernest
1660-85    William of    1685-8        Elector of
       Orange                             Hanover

WILLIAM III = MARY II        ANNE     GEORGE I
1688-1702     1688-94        1702-14    (see Table V)

The Royal Arms of William III
and Mary II

The Royal Arms of Queen Anne

Table IV.

lion seated full-fronted on the Royal Crown with a similar
crown on its head, holding in the right forepaw a sword in
proper colours and in the left a gold sceptre. Above this crest
was placed the motto, *In defens.*

G

At James I's accession the supporters of the Royal Arms took the form that has continued to this day, namely on the dexter side a crowned lion gardant of gold, for England, and on the sinister side a white unicorn with gold horn, hoofs, mane and tufts, having about its neck a gold coronet of crosses formy and fleurs-de-lis and attached thereto a gold chain, for Scotland. However, in Scotland, just as the quarters of the royal shield were rearranged, the position of the supporters was changed so as to place the unicorn on the dexter side, and a crown was placed upon its head as well as the coronet round its neck.

The crowned red and white rose introduced by the Tudors continued to be a Royal Badge of England. A crowned thistle was the badge of Scotland, and sometimes the rose and thistle were shown joined under one crown.

71. Arms of the Commonwealth, 1649–60.

During the Commonwealth the Royal Arms were replaced by the shield illustrated in Fig. 71. This bore the red cross of St George on white in the first and fourth quarters, the white saltire of St Andrew on blue in the second, and the gold harp of Ireland on blue in the third; and in the centre of the shield an escutcheon bearing the personal arms of the Lord Protector, Oliver Cromwell, Sable, a lion rampant argent. On the Great Seal of England dated 1655 this shield appeared

surmounted by a helm bearing the Royal Crest and supported by the lion and dragon as used by the later Tudor
sovereigns.

William III and Mary II, as joint Sovereigns, both bore
the Royal Arms in the form used by the earlier Stuart Kings,
but William added in the centre of the shield an escutcheon
of his own arms of Nassau—Azure, semy of gold billets (oblong
figures) and a lion rampant or. During their joint reign their
arms were impaled on one shield, but when Mary died her
arms were removed and William continued to bear the Royal
Arms with the Nassau escutcheon. At his death this escutcheon
was removed, and Anne bore the Stuart Royal Arms until
1707.

In that year the union of the Kingdoms of England and
Scotland took place. Anne was now Queen not of three
separate realms, but of two, namely Great Britain and Ireland. The merging of England and Scotland into the United
Kingdom of Great Britain was reflected in the Royal Arms
by impaling the arms of England and Scotland in the first
and fourth quarters, those of France being placed in the
second, and those of Ireland in the third, as shown in Table
IV. The Royal Arms continued in this form until 1714.

## The House of Hanover

On the accession of George I a further change in the Royal
Arms became necessary because he was not only King of
Great Britain and Ireland but also Elector of Hanover.
Accordingly the arms of Hanover were placed in the fourth
quarter of the shield. These were—Party per chevron and
the chief per pale; 1, Gules, two gold lions passant gardant
(Brunswick); 2, Or, semy of hearts gules, a lion rampant
azure (Luneburg); 3, Gules, a horse courant argent (West-
phalia); and over all an escutcheon gules charged with the
golden crown of Charlemagne. The arms in this form were
borne by George II and by George III until 1801.

In that year further changes took place in the Royal Arms

# HOUSE OF HANOVER

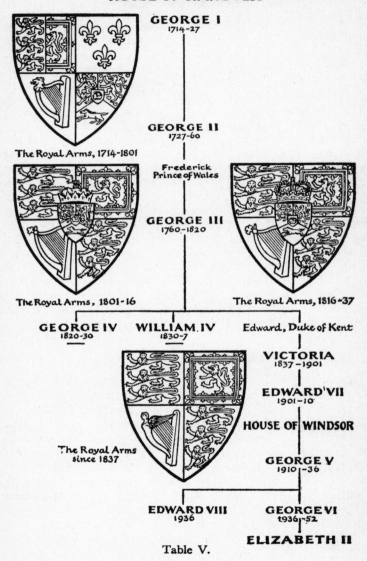

**GEORGE I**
1714-27

The Royal Arms, 1714-1801

**GEORGE II**
1727-60

Frederick
Prince of Wales

**GEORGE III**
1760-1820

The Royal Arms, 1801-16

The Royal Arms, 1816~37

**GEORGE IV**
1820-30

**WILLIAM IV**
1830-7

Edward, Duke of Kent

**VICTORIA**
1837-1901

**EDWARD VII**
1901-10

**HOUSE OF WINDSOR**

The Royal Arms
since 1837

**GEORGE V**
1910-36

**EDWARD VIII**
1936

**GEORGE VI**
1936-52

**ELIZABETH II**

Table V.

to mark the union with Ireland resulting in the United Kingdom of Great Britain and Ireland. After 460 years the arms of France were removed from the shield. They had become meaningless since the loss of Calais, our last French possession, in the reign of Mary I, and more so since the old realm of France represented by the fleurs-de-lis had ceased to exist. In the new shield the arms of England were placed in the first and fourth quarters, those of Scotland in the second, and those of Ireland in the third. Hanover, not being part of the United Kingdom, was represented by its arms on an escutcheon in the centre of the shield. Above this escutcheon was placed an Electoral Bonnet, but in 1816 when Hanover became a kingdom this was replaced by a Royal Crown. The arms are illustrated in Table V.

As Queen Victoria did not succeed to the throne of Hanover, the crowned escutcheon was removed on her accession in 1837, and the Royal Arms reached their present form.

Through all these changes the crest, supporters and motto remained the same as they were in Stuart times, and the shield was encircled by the Garter. For a time the practice of using separate Royal Arms in Scotland lapsed, but this has since been revived and in Scotland the Queen bears *Quarterly, 1 and 4, Scotland, 2, England, 3, Ireland*; with the Scottish crest as described above, and the unicorn supporter on the dexter side. The unicorn is crowned and upholds the banner of St Andrew, while the lion on the sinister side has a banner of St George. Above the crest is placed the motto, *In defens*. The shield is encircled by the collar of the Order of the Thistle, with the badge hanging from it.

## The House of Windsor

Although Queen Victoria did not succeed to the crown of Hanover, she was a Hanoverian by descent and ranks as the last Sovereign of the House of Hanover. Her son Edward VII was of the House of Saxe-Coburg and Gotha, this being the family of his father, the Prince Consort. George V was also of this House, but in 1915, during the first World War, he proclaimed that the dynasty was to be known as the House of Windsor.

As the Royal Arms are Arms of Dominion and not personal arms, a reigning Queen does not impale her husband's arms on the royal shield, but where it is desired to represent both the Sovereign and her Consort their separate achievements may be placed side by side.

Members of the Royal Family bear the Royal Arms with appropriate differences, and unlike private families these are borne by ladies, because none but the Sovereign may bear the undifferenced Royal Arms. These differences always consist of labels—a plain white label for the Sovereign's eldest son, and a white label charged with various emblems for the other sons and daughters. Thus the present Queen, before she came to the throne, bore the Royal Arms with a white label charged on the middle point with a red rose surmounted by a white rose, and with a red cross of St George on each of the other points. Princess Margaret's label is white and bears on the middle point a thistle and on each of the others a combined red and white rose. George V's eldest son when Prince of Wales bore a plain white label, which he removed on coming to the throne as Edward VIII. On his abdication the label was replaced and charged with a Royal Crown to show that he had been King.

The frontispiece to this book shows in colour the full achievement of the Royal Arms including the shield encircled by the Garter, the helm and mantling bearing the crest, the supporters, and the motto *Dieu et mon Droit*, with the national emblems of the united red and white rose for England, the thistle for Scotland and the shamrock for Ireland forming the base of the design. Some versions of the Royal Arms are simpler than this. You will sometimes see the helm, mantling and crest omitted and in their place the Royal Crown (without the lion standing on it) set above the shield. Sometimes the supporters and motto are omitted and the design consists only of the shield, Garter and Crown.

The Royal Crown shown in heraldry consists of a jewelled circlet set with alternate crosses formy and fleurs-de-lis with two pearl-studded arches rising from behind the crosses and supporting a ball surmounted by a cross. Inside the crown is a scarlet cap with an ermine edge which appears below the jewelled circlet. In some representations of the Crown the cap is omitted. The Crown has generally taken this form for the last five hundred years, but the height and shape of the arches has varied. In the present reign they are slightly dipped at the centre. The coronet of the Prince of Wales is similar to the Sovereign's Crown except that it has only one arch.

## Royal Beasts

The various heraldic creatures used as badges and supporters in Plantagenet and Tudor times are still part of the insignia of the Sovereign, though they no longer appear in the Royal Achievement of Arms and are only used for historic purposes. Some of them are to be seen at Windsor, Hampton Court and Kew Gardens.

On the buttresses of St George's Chapel, Windsor Castle, a series of Royal Beasts was set up in Tudor times, denoting Henry VIII's descent from Edward III through various lines (see Tables II and III). In the course of time these beasts became dilapidated and were removed, but in 1925 they were replaced, and if you go to Windsor you can see the following:

A crowned lion with the arms of England, for Edward III.

An heraldic antelope with the Royal Arms, 1340–1405, for Henry IV.

A swan with the arms of Bohun (Azure, a bend argent between two gold cotices (narrow bendlets), and six lions rampant or), for Henry IV's Queen, Mary de Bohun.

An heraldic panther with the arms of Eton College (Sable, three lilies argent, a chief per pale azure with a gold fleur-de-lis and gules with a gold lion of England—Fig. 97), for Henry VI and his foundation.

A yale with the arms of Beaufort (Quarterly France Modern and England within a bordure compony argent and azure—Fig. 98), for the Beaufort line from John of Gaunt.

A dragon of Wales with a Tudor rose charged with the Beaufort portcullis.

A falcon with the arms of England, for Edward III.

A hart with a shield charged with *planta genista*, for Richard II.

A bull of Clarence with a rose amid rays of the sun, for the descent through Edward IV from Lionel, Duke of Clarence.

A dragon of Ulster with the arms of De Burgh, Earl of Ulster (Or, a cross gules), for the wife of Lionel, Duke of Clarence.

A lion of March with the arms of Mortimer (Barry or and azure, an escutcheon argent, on a chief or two pallets between two gyrons (triangular figures) azure), for the Mortimer Earls of March.

A greyhound of Richmond with the arms of Nevill (Gules, a saltire argent).

On the bridge at Hampton Court there are ten Royal Beasts erected in 1910 to replace the ones which had disappeared. These commemorated the marriage of Henry VIII and Jane Seymour. Here you will see a lion, dragon, greyhound, yale, panther, bull and unicorn supporting shields bearing the arms and badges of King Henry and Queen Jane. In this series the unicorn is not the Scottish royal beast but a creature from the insignia of the Seymour family.

For the coronation of Queen Elizabeth II ten heraldic creatures, each bearing an escutcheon charged with royal arms or badges, were fashioned in plaster, and appropriately coloured, to stand outside Westminster Abbey. The originals are preserved at Hampton Court, and copies have been made in stone (without colours) and set up in front of the Palm House in Kew Gardens (Fig. 72). These beasts and the insignia they bear are as follows:—

72. Three of the Queen's beasts in Kew
Gardens.

The lion of England royally crowned, with the Royal Arms
of Queen Elizabeth II.

The griffin of Edward III with the badge of the present
Royal House of Windsor, viz. the Round Tower of
Windsor Castle with the Royal Banner flying from the
turret; above it the Royal Crown, and on each side a
branch of oak.

The falcon of the Plantagenets, with the Yorkist badge of
a white falcon within a gold fetterlock, for the Queen's
descent from the House of York.

The black bull of Clarence, with the Royal Arms, 1405 to
1603, for the Queen's descent from Lionel, Duke of
Clarence, and her succession to the Plantagenet and
Tudor Sovereigns.

The lion of March with the white rose of York within rays
of the sun, for the Queen's descent through the House of
York from the Mortimer Earls of March.

The spotted yale of the Beauforts with the crowned portcullis of Henry VII, from whom the Queen is descended
through his daughter, Margaret.

The greyhound of Richmond with the crowned Tudor rose, also representing the Queen's descent from Henry VII.

The dragon of Wales with the arms of the Principality of Wales (Quarterly or and gules, four lions passant gardant counterchanged), for the Queen's descent through Henry VII from the former Princes of Wales.

The Scottish unicorn with the Royal Arms of Scotland, for the Queen's descent from the Kings of Scotland.

The white horse of Hanover with the Royal Arms, 1714 to 1801, for the Queen's descent from the House of Hanover.

73. Personal Flag of Queen Elizabeth II.

## Royal Flags

The Royal Banner, consisting of the Royal Arms in the form of a flag, is flown over the place where the Queen is in residence, and at the masthead of a ship when she is on board. It is also displayed on the car or aircraft in which she travels on official occasions. However, as the Royal Arms are associated particularly with the United Kingdom of Great Britain and Northern Ireland, it is inappropriate that they should be displayed when Her Majesty visits her other realms, and also those countries of the British Commonwealth of Nations (such as India and Pakistan) which recognize her not as their Queen but as Head of the Commonwealth. Accordingly in 1960 Her Majesty adopted a personal flag to be displayed when the Royal Banner of the United Kingdom is unsuitable, and she first used it during her visit to India and Pakistan in 1961. The new flag is blue edged with gold and bears the Queen's initial E with the Royal Crown above it, the whole within a chaplet of roses, all in gold (Fig. 73). The number of roses in the chaplet is not mentioned in the official description of the flag, but, as the illustration shows, there are in fact eleven roses, and it is interesting to note that this corresponds with the number of sovereign and independent states within the British Commonwealth when the flag was designed. In this flag the Crown is not a symbol of government, as it is in Great Britain. It stands for Her Majesty's personal rank. When she visits the republics within the Commonwealth she is still a Queen, though not the Queen of those countries, and it is therefore proper for her to display a flag containing the crown as the emblem of her royal dignity.

Other members of the Royal Family have banners bearing their arms which are flown over their houses and on cars. The banner of Queen Elizabeth the Queen Mother contains

74. Banner of Queen Elizabeth the Queen Mother.

the Royal Arms of George VI impaling the quartered coats of Lyon and Bowes: Argent, a lion rampant within the tressure of Scotland all azure, for Lyon, and Ermine, three long bows erect gules, for Bowes (Fig. 74). It will be noted that the arms of Lyon are identical in design, but not in colour, with the Royal Arms of Scotland. The lion, of course, alludes to the family name, and the royal tressure was added to denote their descent from a daughter of King Robert II of Scotland.

The banner of Prince Philip, Duke of Edinburgh, displays his arms, which are: Quarterly; 1, Or, semy of hearts gules, three lions passant azure with gold crowns, for Denmark; 2, Azure, a cross argent, for Greece; 3, Argent, two pallets sable, for Mountbatten; and 4, Argent, on a rock proper a castle with three towers of sable stones outlined in silver, each tower topped by a vane gules, for Edinburgh (Fig. 81). The quarters represent Prince Philip's descent, through his father, from the Royal Houses of Denmark and Greece, and through his mother from the family of Mountbatten (formerly Battenburg), while the fourth quarter contains the arms of Edinburgh with reference to his dukedom.

We are all familiar with the Union Flag, commonly called the 'Union Jack'. This is usually regarded as a national flag, and by long-standing custom ordinary citizens fly it over their houses and premises at national celebrations. It is, however, strictly speaking a Royal Flag, which ought only to be flown on Government property, though the authorities raise no objection to its being displayed on private property as a sign of loyalty. At sea, however, where the use of flags is more strictly regulated, the Union Flag may only be flown by the Royal Navy, though British subjects may fly a red flag with the union in the corner—the 'Red Ensign'.

The Union Flag in its present form, incorporating the cross of St George (for England), and the saltires of St Andrew (for Scotland) and St Patrick (for Ireland), dates from the union of Great Britain and Ireland in 1801. Before that, from the Union of England and Scotland in 1707, the flag consisted only of the combined cross of St George and

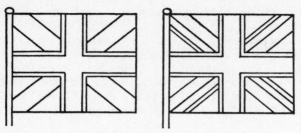

75. The Union Flag, past and present.

saltire of St Andrew, and you may often see this in eighteenth century paintings of ships of the Royal Navy (Fig. 75).

When the second Union Flag was designed the red saltire of St Patrick was at first placed along the centre of the white saltire of St Andrew, but the Scots objected to this because they thought it made their part of the flag merely a background to the Irish emblem. Accordingly the red saltire was moved out of the centre line, so as to have a broad white piece on one side and a narrow one on the other side. The broad parts of the white diagonals represent St Andrew's saltire, while the narrow parts are regarded as the background to St Patrick's. As the union with Scotland took place before that with Ireland, St Andrew's saltire takes precedence of St Patrick's, and this is shown by the way the flag is mounted on its staff. It is flown so that at the top corner nearest the staff the broad white diagonal is uppermost. If the narrower portion is uppermost the flag is upside down.

## Coinage and Stamps

The coinage of the present reign is particularly interesting in its use of the Royal Arms and Badges. Following a tradition going back to the reign of Edward VI, the reverse side of the half crown bears a shield of the Royal Arms. On the crown piece the quarters for England, Scotland and Ireland are placed on separate shields, with the English rose, the

Scottish thistle, the Irish shamrock and the Welsh leek between them, and the Royal Crown in the centre of the coin. This is the first appearance in our coinage of the leek as an emblem of Wales. There are two designs for the reverse of the shilling, one consisting of the English quarter of the Royal Arms, and the other of the Scottish quarter, each on a shield. Above each shield there is a Royal Crown, and if you compare them closely you will see a slight difference between the crowns. On the English design the crown is of the familiar type with the arches rising from behind the crosses formy, while on the Scottish design the arches spring from behind the fleurs-de-lis, a detail which gives the crown a slight resemblance to the Crown of Scotland preserved at Edinburgh Castle. The two types of shilling continue a practice begun in the reign of King George VI, when some shillings bore on the reverse the Royal Crest of England and others that of Scotland.

On some other coins Royal Badges are used. The florin minted in the present reign bears a double rose within a wreath of thistles, shamrock and leeks, while all four of these national emblems are intertwined in the design on the sixpenny piece. The Tudor badge of a crowned portcullis has been revived for use on the reverse of the threepenny bit, perhaps with the idea of linking the second Queen Elizabeth with the first, in whose reign the portcullis appeared on the halfpenny.

The rose, thistle and shamrock are also seen on the stamps, together with a daffodil which is an alternative to the leek as an emblem of Wales. On the half-crown and five-shilling stamps of George VI's reign the Royal Arms appear encircled by the Garter, surmounted by the Crown, and supported by the lion and the unicorn, with the Sovereign's head above them.

76. Funeral Hatchments.

# 7. Heraldry in Churches

HERALDRY is abundant in the cathedrals and churches throughout Great Britain. It is to be found on tombs and monuments of all periods, in stained-glass windows, and carved in stone and wood on walls, roofs, stalls and screens, and on the sides of fonts, while shields of a religious character may often be seen on altar hangings and other furnishings of the sanctuary. In the chapels of the Orders of Chivalry, such as St George's at Windsor, there is a colourful display of heraldic banners.

Many churches dating from the fifteenth century or earlier contain effigies of men in armour, either sculptured in marble or some other stone, or consisting of a flat metal plate (or *brass*) cut to the shape of a man and incised so as to show his features and the details of his armour and equipment. In the older effigies the man is shown lying on his back with his hands together as though in prayer, and with a lion, or sometimes a hound, lying at his feet. Some later effigies consist of a kneeling figure.

The armour represented in the effigy is, of course, that which was worn during the man's lifetime and varies with the period. Effigies made in the thirteenth or early part of the fourteenth century are shown in mail—that is, inter-linked iron rings, sometimes called 'chain mail'—in some cases with metal plates protecting the knees. They are girded with their swords and carry their shields on their left arms. The shields are usually emblazoned with their arms, though where these were only painted and not cut in the stone or metal, they have in some cases disappeared. On some effigies of this period the arms also appear on the surcoats, though here again sometimes only traces of colour remain. Occasionally the knight's arms are also shown on *ailettes*—square plates projecting from the shoulders—as in the brass of Sir Roger de Trumpington at Trumpington near Cambridge (Fig. 77). This brass also shows how a knight was sometimes represented resting his head on his helm.

In the early part of the fourteenth century it became the custom to strengthen mail with metal plates on the shoulders and upper arms and on the shins and feet, and the use of this was gradually extended. Edward, Prince of Wales (the 'Black Prince'), who died in 1376, is represented on his monument at Canterbury in armour consisting of plate ex-cept for the mail laced to his steel cap and covering his neck and shoulders (Fig. 78). As a result of the strengthening of mail with plate knights found the shield less necessary as a means of defence (except when jousting), and between 1340 and 1360 the shield on the knight's arm gradually disappeared from effigies. They still had their armorial bearings on their surcoats, and the arms were also shown on small shields on the sides of the monument or, in the case of a brass, above the knight's head. When the knight was represented with his head resting on his helm, this often bore his crest, as may be seen in the effigy of the Black Prince.

Early in the fifteenth century complete plate armour was introduced, though mail was sometimes still worn under it. Knights are still seen in surcoats emblazoned with their arms, and these sometimes consisted of quartered coats, as on the effigy at Arundel of John Fitzalan, Earl of Arundel, who died

77. Brass of Sir Roger de Trump-ington, at Trumpington, Cambridge.

78. Effigy of Edward, Prince of Wales (the Black Prince), at Canterbury.

H

in 1435 (Fig. 79). He quartered the gold lion on red of Fitz-alan with the arms of Maltravers—Sable, fretty gold—because he held the barony of Maltravers through the marriage of one of his ancestors with the heiress of Lord Maltravers. Round his neck is a collar consisting of letters S, which was worn by some adherents to the house of Lancaster. The Earl's badge, a white horse, lies at his feet.

About the middle of the fifteenth century surcoats began to go out of fashion, but towards the end of the century, and in the early Tudor period, some knights are represented in tabards—that is, loose tunics with short sleeves embroidered with their arms, in some cases consisting of six or eight quarterings.

Ladies are sometimes shown wearing heraldic garments. Some fourteenth-century effigies of ladies represent them in dresses on which their husbands' arms are impaled with their own. In fifteenth- and sixteenth-century examples the heraldic garment takes the form of a cloak on which the arms of husband and wife are displayed, sometimes with a number of quarterings. Fig. 80 shows Lady Gascoigne, first wife of Sir William Gascoigne, on a brass dated 1540 in Cardington Church, Bedfordshire. She has on her kirtle the arms of Winter, her father's family—Ermine, a lion rampant sable charged on the shoulder with a molet gold for difference. Her mantle bears her husband's arms: Quarterly, 1 and 4, Argent, on a pale sable a conger eel's head erect or, charged with a molet azure for difference, for Gascoigne; 2, Gules, three picks argent, for Picot; 3, Quarterly or and gules, a bend gules, for Beauchamp of Bedford.

On many monuments of the fifteenth century and later you will see a number of shields round the sides of the tomb or on the canopy above it, bearing the arms of the person commemorated, and those of his wife, and also their arms combined on the same shield, either by impalement or by escutcheon of pretence. In some cases the monument also bears the arms of families from which the person was indirectly descended. In the sixteenth and seventeenth cen-

79. Effigy of John Fitzalan,
Earl of Arundel, at Arundel.

80. Lady Gascoigne, on a
brass at Cardington.

turies many monuments of important people were elaborate pieces of architecture, rich in heraldry. They were often surmounted by three shields, the outer ones displaying the arms and quarterings of the husband and wife separately, while the middle one showed these combined, sometimes consisting of an impaled shield with eight, ten or twelve quarterings in each half. In the case of a peer the shield is flanked by his supporters and has his coronet, and sometimes his crest, above it; while his badges are worked into the decoration of the monument. Several examples of the richly heraldic monuments of this period may be seen in Westminster Abbey, notably that of Sir Henry Carey, Lord Hunsdon, who died in 1596.

In many old churches you will see funeral hatchments hanging on the wall. The word *hatchment* is derived from *achievement* of arms, and is applied to the arms of a person who is dead, these being painted on a lozenge-shaped piece of canvas or wood enclosed in a black frame. It was formerly the custom, when a member of an important family died, to hang a hatchment painted with his or her arms outside the house as a sign of mourning. After the period of mourning the hatchment was removed to the church where the person was buried, to serve as a memorial while a monument was being erected, and in some cases the hatchment remained on the wall of the church permanently. In the case of a bachelor the arms were painted on a shield, usually with his crest above it, though sometimes a skull was put in place of the crest. An unmarried woman's arms were placed on a lozenge, with no crest but often with a knot of ribbon in its place. In both these cases the whole of the background of the hatchment was painted black.

If the hatchment related to the death of a married person, the combined arms of husband and wife were painted on a shield. The crest was included if the hatchment commemorated the husband, but not if it referred to the wife. When a man died leaving a widow the dexter half of the background was painted black, the other half being left white. If the wife died in her husband's lifetime, the sinister side of her hatchment was painted black and the dexter left white. Accordingly in the case of a hatchment bearing the combined arms of husband and wife, you can tell which one it commemorates by whether there is a crest or not, and you can also tell whether the husband survived the wife, or vice versa, by the treatment of the background.

Fig. 76 shows two hatchments formerly in Chelsea Old Church. In each case the arms are the same—a quartered shield bearing an escutcheon of pretence, showing that the arms are those of married persons, the wife being an heiress. The first hatchment has no crest, but a pair of cherubs appear in its place. From this, and from the fact that the sinister side of the background is black, we know that the hatchment refers to the death of a married woman, while the white background on the dexter side shows that her husband survived her. The second hatchment has a crest, showing it is that of a man. As the background is all black we know that his wife predeceased him.

In the hatchment of a bishop, who impaled the arms of his see with his personal arms, the background behind the arms of the see was left white, the other half being black, because though the man died the see continued. The same applies to kings of arms, masters of colleges, and others entitled to impale official and personal arms.

In St George's Chapel, Windsor Castle, you may see the heraldic banners of the Knights of the Garter hanging above their stalls, together with helms bearing their crests, while the Royal Banner hangs over the Sovereign's stall. The banners are those of the knights of the Order for the time being, and when a knight dies his banner is removed. On the backs of the stalls are plates bearing the arms of the knights who have formerly occupied them. A few of these plates date from the fourteenth century and a number from the fifteenth century, the rest being more recent. They are fine examples of heraldic art at various periods and a valuable source of information about heraldry. Fig. 82 shows the oldest remaining

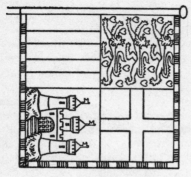

81. Banner of the Duke of Edinburgh.

82. Stall-plate of Ralph, Lord Bassett, Knight of the Garter, at Windsor.

stall-plate—that of Ralph, Lord Bassett, a Knight of the Garter from 1368 to 1390, whose arms were, Or, three piles (wedge-shaped figures) meeting in base gules, a quarter ermine. The boar's head forming his crest was black and it rose from a gold crest-coronet, and the mantling was also black.

The banners and stall plates of the Knights of the Bath are to be seen in Henry VII's Chapel in Westminster Abbey and those of the Knights Grand Cross of St Michael and St George in the Order's chapel at St Paul's Cathedral. In 1960 a chapel for the Order of the British Empire was also established in St Paul's, and the banners of the Sovereign and members of the Royal Family who belong to the Order are hung there. Fig. 81 shows the banner of the Duke of Edinburgh, Grand Master of the Order.

The Orders of Chivalry and their insignia are dealt with in Chapter 4.

83. Royal Arms of Queen Elizabeth I in Kenning-
hall Church.

In many old churches you will find a painting of the Royal
Arms as they were in former times. The practice of displaying
the Royal Arms in churches goes back to the time when
Henry VIII declared himself Head of the Church of England.
Those put up in his reign were removed, and most of them
destroyed, when his Catholic daughter Mary came to the
throne. The practice was resumed under Elizabeth, and Fig.
83 shows an example surviving from her time, but most of
the Royal Arms put up in her reign, and those of her two
successors, were removed during the Commonwealth. Consequently few of the paintings of the Royal Arms which exist
in churches today date from earlier than the time of Charles II.
The form of the arms will show you the period they belong
to (see Chapter 6, on Royal Heraldry). The paintings often
bear the initial and number of the monarch in whose reign
they were made, e.g. C II for Charles II, G I for George I,

etc. However, you will sometimes find the Royal Arms of the
Stuart period accompanied by the initial of one of the
Georges, owing to the fact that the church authorities did not
trouble to have the arms repainted in the form they took in
Hanoverian times but merely had the Sovereign's initial
altered. Some of these paintings were done by local craftsmen
without much knowledge of heraldry, and are incorrect in
certain details.

Shields bearing religious emblems, such as the five wounds
of Christ (Fig. 84) and the cross, nails, and crown of thorns,
are frequently found in old churches, and also the arms
assigned to the saint in whose name the church is dedicated.
The emblems of saints most frequently found as patrons of
churches in Great Britain are:—

St Mary the Virgin: Azure, a heart gules with gold wings,
the heart pierced by a silver sword with a gold hilt; and
Azure, three lilies proper standing in a gold vase.

St Andrew: Azure, a saltire argent.

St Edmund, King and Martyr: Azure, three open crowns
or; and Azure, an open crown or pierced by two gold
arrows saltirewise. The latter refers to the fact that St
Edmund, King of the East Angles, was shot to death
with arrows by the Danes.

St Edward the Confessor: Azure, a cross patonce between
five martlets (or doves) all gold (Fig. 23). These form
part of the arms of Westminster Abbey, with the addition of a gold chief bearing the Royal Arms of France
and England quarterly between two Tudor roses
(Fig. 85).

St George: Argent, a cross gules.

St James: Azure, three escallops or.

St Lawrence: Argent, a gridiron sable.

St Margaret: Azure, a gold dragon's head pierced through
the jaws by a gold cross.

St Michael: Argent, a cross pommy gules.

St Patrick: Argent, a saltire gules.

84. The Five          85. Westminster        86. See of
Wounds of Christ.         Abbey.              Winchester.

St Paul: Gules, two gold swords saltirewise. These arms,
    with blades of the swords silver, are borne by the See of
    London.
St Peter: Gules, two keys saltirewise, one gold and the
    other silver.

In the case of churches dedicated in the joint names of St
Peter and St Paul a shield may be seen bearing the two keys
with the sword thrust between them, as in the arms of the
See of Winchester (Fig. 86). Here the field is red, the upper
key is gold and the other silver, and the sword has a silver
blade and a gold hilt.

The arms of the ecclesiastical province or diocese in which
the parish lies may be seen in some churches. The arms of the
See of Canterbury, dating from the fourteenth century, are:
Azure, an archbishop's crozier with a silver staff and a gold
cross surmounted by a pall argent edged and fringed with
gold and charged with four crosses formy fitchy (i.e. having
their lower limbs pointed) sable (Fig. 87). The arms of the
See of York are: Gules, two silver keys saltirewise and in
chief a gold crown with a pointed cap (Fig. 88).

For religious festivals and national occasions flags may be
seen flying from church towers. Some cathedrals and important churches like Westminster Abbey have several flags for

87. See of            88. See of
Canterbury.           York.

use on various occasions, one bearing the arms of the see and
another the emblems of the patron saint. The flag usually
flown over a parish church is white with the cross of St
George and in the first quarter a shield bearing the arms of
the see in which the parish is situated.

While most of our ancient cathedrals contain many interesting examples of heraldic insignia, special mention must
be made of Canterbury, where in the vaulting of the Great
Cloister you may see more than eight hundred shields bearing
the arms of notabilities who contributed to the building of
the cloister in the fifteenth century. These shields were
carved in stone and coloured. In the course of time they became grimy and dilapidated, but in the present century they
have been restored and repainted, and they now form a
valuable and fascinating record of medieval arms and the
heraldic art of the period. The shields are illustrated and
described in a volume on *The Heraldry of Canterbury Cathedral*,
published by the Friends of the Cathedral.

*Heraldry in Westminster Abbey* is the subject of a booklet (by
the present author) on sale at the Abbey.

89. Oxford
University.

90. Cambridge
University.

91. London
University.

# 8. Arms of Universities, Colleges and Schools

The Universities of Oxford and Cambridge had their beginnings in the twelfth century, but it was not until the thirteenth century that the organization of students in colleges began. The universities and their colleges needed seals for official purposes. In the case of the colleges the design on the seal sometimes included the figure of the founder and his or her shield of arms, and in due course the college began to use these arms, or a variation of them, as its own. Some later foundations were granted armorial bearings by the Kings of Arms.

The arms of Oxford University made their appearance on its seal in the early part of the fifteenth century. They are: Azure, between three gold crowns an open book proper, its binding gules and the edges of the pages gold, having on the dexter side seven gold seals, and the pages inscribed with the words, *Dominus illuminatio mea* ('The Lord is my light', from Psalm 27). The number of seals is that of the book described in Revelations, Chapter 5. The three gold crowns on blue are from the arms attributed to St Edmund, the East Anglian King and Martyr, who in the middle ages was revered

113

92. Balliol,          93. Merton,          94. Christ Church,
   Oxford.              Oxford.              Oxford.

equally with St George and St Edward the Confessor as a
national saint (Fig. 89).

University College, Oxford, historically dates from 1249,
but there is a groundless tradition that it descends from a
school founded by King Alfred. It bears the arms which are
principally associated with Edward the Confessor (Fig. 23)
but which were sometimes used also to represent King Alfred.

Balliol College, Oxford, founded between 1263 and 1268,
bears the impaled arms of its two founders, Devorguilla,
daughter of Alan Lord of Galloway, and her husband, John
Lord Balliol of Barnard Castle. The arms are: Azure, a lion
rampant argent crowned or (for Devorguilla), impaling Gules
an orle argent (for Balliol) (Fig. 92). It will be seen that Devorguilla's arms are placed on the dexter side, which is usually
the husband's side of an impaled shield, but in this case her
arms were given precedence because her lordship was more
important than her husband's. It will also be noticed that
only half the Balliol orle is shown, this practice being usual
with orles, tressures and bordures in impaled shields owing
to the difficulty of including the whole of these charges in
half a shield. Wadham College (founded in 1612) also bears
the impaled arms of its founders (Fig. 37).

Merton College, Oxford, uses the arms of Walter de
Merton, Chancellor of England and later Bishop of Rochester,
who founded the College in 1264. The arms are: Or, three

chevronels parted palewise, the first and third azure and gules and the middle one gules and azure. These arms are sometimes shown impaled on the sinister side with those of the See of Rochester: Argent, on a saltire gules a gold escallop (Fig. 93).

Oriel College, Oxford, though founded in 1324 by Adam de Brome, bears the Royal Arms of Edward II (Gules, three lions passant gardant or) differenced by a bordure engrailed argent, because that King permitted himself to be named as its founder. On the other hand Queen's College, nominally founded by Philippa, Queen of Edward III, bears the arms of its actual founder, who was her chaplain, Robert of Eglesfield. These are: Argent, three eagles displayed gules, on the first a pierced molet of six points gold. The eagles, of course, allude to his name.

Most of the other colleges at Oxford bear arms based upon those of their founders, and in some cases their shields also include the arms of those who have refounded or endowed the college. The arms of Christ Church are interesting as an heraldic record of the career of its first founder, Cardinal Thomas Wolsey. They are: Sable, on a cross engrailed argent a lion passant gules between four leopards' faces azure, and on a chief or a rose gules between two Cornish choughs proper (Fig. 94). The cross from the arms of the Uffords and the leopards' faces from those of the De la Poles, successively earls of Suffolk, represent the county where Wolsey was born. The lion refers to Pope Leo X who made him a Cardinal. The choughs are from the arms of St Thomas Becket, Wolsey's name-saint, and the rose alludes to his position as a royal minister.

The arms of the University of Cambridge dating from 1573, are: Gules, on a cross ermine between four gold lions of England a closed book gules, edged, clasped and studded with gold (Fig. 90). The oldest college at Cambridge is Peterhouse, founded in 1284 by Hugh of Balsham, Bishop of Ely. His arms were, Or, four pallets gules, while those of the See of Ely were, Gules, three crowns or. The College com-

95. Peterhouse,
Cambridge.

96. King's,
Cambridge.

97. Eton
College.

bines these by bearing Balsham's arms within a bordure
gules charged with eight gold crowns (Fig. 95). Jesus College
was also founded (in 1496) by a Bishop of Ely, namely John
Alcock. His arms were, Argent, a fess sable between three
cocks' heads erased sable with combs and wattles gules.
(*Erased*, from *arraché*, means that the heads are torn off at the
neck.) The college bears these within a bordure gules charged
with eight gold crowns. The three crowns in the arms of the
See of Ely are indirectly connected with the crowns of St
Edmund which we have noted in the arms of Oxford University because Etheldreda, the foundress of the first Abbey at
Ely, was the daughter of an East Anglian King.

   Cambridge has several royal foundations. King's College,
founded in 1441 by Henry VI, bears: Sable, three silver roses,
on a chief parted palewise azure and gules a fleur-de-lis and
a lion of England, both gold (Fig. 96). These were granted in
1449, and the grant explained the significance of the charges.
The roses indicated that the College should 'bring forth the
brightest flowers redolent of every kind of knowledge' to the
honour and worship of God and the Virgin Mary, and the
fleur-de-lis and lion were included 'to impart something of
Royal nobility which may declare the work truly Royal and
illustrious'. Eton College, also founded by Henry VI and
dedicated to St Mary, was granted similar arms to those of

98. Arms of Lady Margaret Beaufort, Foundress of
Christ's and St. John's Colleges, Cambridge.

King's College but with white lilies in place of the roses
(Fig. 97).

Queens' College was founded first by Henry VI's Queen,
Margaret of Anjou, and secondly by Elizabeth Woodville,
Queen of Edward IV. Its arms are those of its first foundress
—who quartered the coats of Hungary, Naples, Jerusalem,
Anjou, Barr and Lorraine—within a green border for
difference.

In 1337 Edward III founded King's Hall at Cambridge,
and in 1546 Henry VIII joined this with another old foundation called Michaelhouse and increased their endowments
so as to form Trinity College. The arms of this College are,
Argent, a chevron gules between three red roses and on a
chief gules a gold lion of England between two books, also
gold (Fig. 99).

Two Cambridge colleges were founded by Lady Margaret
Beaufort, mother of Henry VII, namely Christ's (1505) and
Saint John's (1511). Both bear her arms: Quarterly France
Modern and England within a bordure compony argent and
azure. Fig. 98 is drawn from a carving of her arms at Christ's
College, where the shield is supported by the Beaufort yales
and has a demi-eagle rising from a coronet above it.

99. Trinity,
Cambridge.

100. Corpus Christi,
Cambridge.

101. Gonville and
Caius, Cambridge.

Religious emblems form the arms of Corpus Christi Col-
lege, Cambridge, founded in 1352 by two guilds of townsmen—the Guilds of Corpus Christi and of the Blessed Virgin
Mary. The arms are, Quarterly, 1 and 4 Gules, a pelican
in its piety argent; 2 and 3 Azure, three lily flowers argent
(Fig. 100). The pelican 'in its piety' is shown feeding its
young with blood drawn from its own breast, a symbol of the
Eucharist; while the lily flower is an emblem of St Mary.
St Catharine's College, Cambridge, also has a religious
device, its arms being Gules, a gold Catharine wheel, in
allusion to the Patron Saint's martyrdom.

Most of the other Cambridge colleges bear arms based on
those of their founders. The arms of Pembroke College have
already been given as an instance of dimidiated shields
(Fig. 36). The impaled arms of Clare (Or, three chevronels
gules) and De Burgh (Or, a cross gules) within a bordure
sable semy of golden drops are borne by Clare College,
founded in 1338 by Elizabeth de Burgh, heiress of her
brother Gilbert, Earl of Clare. The black border with
golden tear-drops is said to have been added to her arms as
a sign of mourning after the death of her third husband.

The arms of Gonville and Caius College contain an instance of the elaborate and symbolic heraldry of the sixteenth century. The College was first founded in 1348 (as

Gonville Hall) by Edmund Gonville, whose arms were, Argent, on a chevron between two chevronels indented sable three escallops or. It was refounded in 1557 by John Caius, M.D., to whom the following arms were granted: Or, semy of flowers gentil, in chief a sengreen resting on the heads of two serpents erect, their tails bound together, all in their proper colours; the serpents resting on a square green marble stone and supporting between them a book sable edged gules and studded and clasped gold. The symbolism of the arms is explained in the grant, the book betokening learning, the serpents on the stone 'wisdom with grace founded and stayed upon vertue's stable stone', and the sengreen (or house-leek) and flowers gentil 'immortalitie that never shall fade'. The college bears the arms of Gonville impaling those of Caius within a bordure compony argent and sable (Fig. 101).

The red cross of St George from the arms of the City of London together with tokens of royal favour appear in the arms granted to the University of London in 1838. These are: Argent, on a cross gules a united red and white rose within rays of gold ensigned with the Royal Crown proper, and on a chief azure an open book also proper, the clasps gold (Fig. 91).

The arms of Durham University, granted in 1843, contain a cross of a form associated with St Cuthbert, Bishop of Lindisfarne in the seventh century, who is buried in Durham Cathedral, which is dedicated in his name. The arms are, Argent, a cross formy squared at the centre gules, on a canton azure a chevron or between three lions rampant argent (Fig. 103). The arms on the canton are those of Bishop Thomas Hatfield who in 1380 founded Durham College at Oxford, the forerunner of Trinity College. Bishop Hatfield's arms within a bordure ermine are also borne by Hatfield College, Durham. A cross like that in the shield of the University appears with other emblems in the arms of St John's College and St Mary's College, while St Aidan's Society and Bede College bear 'ancient Northumbrian crosses', which are somewhat similar.

I

102. Liverpool       103. Durham       104. Leeds
University.          University.        University.

Several universities bear on their shields emblems from the
arms of the cities in which they stand, often together with a
book. Liverpool University has on blue shield an open book
bound in gold, with white pages inscribed with the words
*Fiat Lux* ('Let there be light') in black letters, between three
cormorants (or livers) each with a strip of laver (seaweed) in
its beak, all proper (Fig. 102). The livers with laver are from
the City arms and allude to its name. Leeds University also
has on a green shield an open book with a gold binding
bearing on its white pages the words *Et augebitur scientia* ('And
knowledge shall be increased', from Daniel xii. 4). In chief
are three silver molets, from the City arms, and in base a
white rose representing Yorkshire (Fig. 104).

Harrow School, founded in 1571 by John Lyon, long used
a lion as a badge. In 1929 the school was granted as arms:
Azure, a lion rampant argent, in dexter chief two arrows
saltirewise points downwards tied with a bow and encircled
with a wreath of laurel all argent (Fig. 105). In addition,
the tied and wreathed arrows were granted to the school as a
badge and may thus be used independently of the arms.
Winchester College which, like Eton, is dedicated to St Mary,
has ancient arms consisting of three white lilies on a black
shield, but it frequently makes use of the arms of its founder,
William of Wykeham, Bishop of Winchester (1324–1404),

105. Harrow
School.

106. Winchester
College.

107. Broxbourne
Grammar School.

which are: Argent, two chevrons sable between three roses
gules with gold centres and sepals vert (Fig. 106). These arms
are also borne by Wykeham's other foundation, New College, Oxford.

Many other schools display the arms of their founders,
quite rightly because this is a way by which their members
are constantly reminded of the honour and gratitude they
owe to their founders. However, it should be noted that unless
such arms have been officially recorded or granted by the
Kings of Arms to the school they are not the property of the
school itself. They are the founder's arms used by the school
commemoratively. In fact comparatively few schools have
obtained grants of arms. Some make use of the shield of an
institution with which they are connected. Thus Westminster
School uses the arms of the Abbey (Fig. 85), Oundle those of
the Grocers' Company, Merchant Taylors' School those of
the Company of that name, and the City of London School
displays the City shield.

The arms of the City of London also appear in the shield
used by Christ's Hospital, with the addition of a chief azure
charged with a white rose between two gold fleurs-de-lis.
Christ's Hospital, or the 'Blue-coat-School', now at Horsham,
was founded in the City of London by Edward VI, and the
civic authorities were made its governors. A number of schools

in different parts of the country are known as 'King Edward. VI Grammar Schools', and some of them display his arms, *Quarterly France Modern and England.* It is commonly believed that these schools were founded, or at least endowed, by Edward VI, but this is not the case. In fact they existed before his time as schools connected with chantries where priests prayed for the souls of their founders. The chantries were abolished in 1548 but some of the schools were permitted to continue. These are called after Edward VI, and display his arms, for no better reason than that his government did not sweep them away.

Many schools controlled by local education authorities use on their caps and blazers and in other ways the arms, or part of the arms, of the county or city in which they are situated. Arms used in this way remain the property of the public body to which they were granted. Schools may be given permission to use them, but they do not thereby become the 'school arms'. Some schools have adopted badges which, while not actually armorial bearings, are heraldic in design. Fig. 107 shows the badge of Broxbourne Grammar School, consisting of the head of a badger, or *brock* on a red background with wavy white and blue bars below representing a *bourne.* The design is enclosed by the antlers of a hart for Hertfordshire.

108. City of London.

# 9. Arms of Counties and Towns

THE councils of many counties, cities and towns, and other bodies connected with local government in Great Britain, have armorial bearings which are used on their seals and documents and may also be seen on town halls and other public buildings. These arms are also often displayed on transport, from the official car of the mayor or chairman of council to vehicles engaged on such matters as refuse-collection. You may think it strange that something which began as a method of distinguishing knights in armour should now be used in such commonplace ways, but this shows that heraldry is still a living thing, and as much part of everyday life as it was in the days of chivalry. A coat of

123

arms painted on the side of a lorry or dust-cart is not only a
welcome decoration on an otherwise prosaic object, but it is
also an indication of the body which owns the vehicle and a
reminder that it, and the men in charge, are engaged upon
work for the benefit of the community represented by the
arms.

In some cases the armorial bearings of a county or town or
other public body consist only of a shield, perhaps with a
motto below it. Many also have crests, and some have supporters. The arms of some old towns have been in use for
four hundred years or more, but most civic arms have been
granted during the last hundred years. County and civic
heraldry is of great interest because it frequently tells in symbolic form something of the history of the locality, the lordships and important families which have been connected
with it, the industries on which its prosperity has been built,
and other features of the community's life. The arms are
legally the property of the council forming the local authority
of the county, town or district, but the inhabitants generally
can take an interest and a pride in them.

London was the first English city to adopt arms. The seal
made for the Mayor of London in 1380 contained, amongst
other emblems, a shield bearing a cross with a sword in the
dexter chief. This shield became the arms of the City of
London, the cross and sword being coloured red on a white
ground. The cross represents the national patron, St George,
and the sword stands for St Paul, the patron saint of the City.
(You may sometimes hear it said that the sword is really the
dagger with which Sir William Walworth slew Wat Tyler,
but this is not so as the arms existed shortly before Tyler's
rebellion.) In the sixteenth century a helm was placed above
the shield, and on it a scalloped plate bearing a red cross
like the one in the arms, but without the sword in the
corner. Later this plate was changed into a dragon's wing,
and the crest of the City became a dragon's wing argent
charged with a cross gules, while two silver dragons with red
crosses on their wings were adopted as supporters (Fig. 108).

109. City of York.     110. City of Canter-     111. City of Lancaster.
                              bury.

These armorial bearings are to be seen at London's Guildhall
and at many other places in the City. On the site of Temple
Bar in Fleet Street there is a pedestal on which is perched a
fine spirited dragon supporting the City arms. Londoners
often refer to this creature as 'the Griffin', but it is really an
heraldic dragon.

York and Lincoln also bear St George's cross on a white
shield, the former with five gold lions of England (Fig. 109)
and the latter with a gold fleur-de-lis on the cross. Lions and
fleurs-de-lis, from the Royal Arms in Plantagenet and Tudor
times, are found in the arms of many old cities and towns.
Canterbury has one gold lion on a red chief in a white shield
bearing three Cornish choughs from the arms of St Thomas
Becket (Fig. 110), and Lancaster's shield is parted fesswise
azure and gules, in chief a fleur-de-lis and in base a lion
of England, both gold (Fig. 111).

In the arms of the Cinque Ports the shield of England is
dimidiated with a blue shield bearing three silver ships' hulls,
so that you have a shield parted palewise gules and azure
with three gold lions passant gardant halved and joined to
the stern ends of three silver ships (Fig. 112). These arms are
borne unchanged by Sandwich and Rye, but Hastings has
the middle lion complete (Fig. 113), while New Romney
omits the hulls and places the three lions of England on a
blue shield. Dover's shield has a red border charged with

112. Cinque Ports.     113. Hastings.     114. Great Yarmouth.

gold lions surrounding St Martin on horseback dividing his
cloak with a beggar. Ramsgate and Margate each have a lion
joined to a hull in their arms to show a connection with the
Cinque Ports, while Great Yarmouth, whose herring fisheries
were formerly controlled by the Ports, has the arms of
England dimidiated with a blue shield containing three
silver herrings, so that the lions appear to be fish-tailed
(Fig. 114).

Lions of England appear in the arms of three counties
which contain royal residences. In the shield of the former
County of London (which included Buckingham Palace,
St James's Palace and the Palace of Westminster), a gold
lion is placed on the cross of St George on a chief argent, the
lower part of the shield being barry wavy azure and argent
representing the Thames (Fig. 115). Norfolk, which contains
Sandringham, has a red chief with a lion of England between
two white ostrich feathers with gold princes' coronets above
them; in the lower part of the shield are the traditional
arms of the first Earl of Norfolk—per pale or and sable with
a bend ermine (Fig. 116). Berkshire has two gold lions passant gardant on blue within an embattled border of ermine
(Fig. 117). The two lions are from the arms attributed to
Henry II (see Table I), and here represent the Norman Kings
who first made Windsor a royal seat, while the embattled
border stands for Windsor Castle. In the arms of the Borough

115. London County     116. Norfolk.     117. Berkshire.

of Windsor (officially called New Windsor) the castle is represented by three silver towers connected by a wall in the base of a shield parted fesswise argent and vert, and above it a silver stag's head with black antlers enclosing a scutcheon of the old Royal Arms, *Quarterly France Modern and England* (Fig. 118).

In Scotland, Perthshire has heraldic distinction as the county containing the ancient royal capital of Scone. The arms of the County contain the red lion rampant within its double tressure of fleurs-de-lis on gold, from the Scottish Royal Arms, differenced by the lion standing on a green mound and brandishing a scimitar, in proper colours, together with a blue canton charged with a representation of the Palace of Scone in silver with a gold Royal Crown above it (Fig. 119). The Royal Crown and other parts of the regalia are seldom found in county or civic heraldry. Where it is desired to include a crown to indicate royal associations one of an antique pattern is generally used. Thus Surrey has in its arms the crown of King Edgar, Egham that of King John (Fig. 137), and Middlesex and other places connected with the Anglo-Saxon Kingdoms have Saxon crowns. An interesting instance of the representation of actual regalia in arms is provided by the shield of Kincardineshire. This is red, charged with the Sword of State and the Sceptre of Scotland in saltire, with the Crown of Scotland in chief and a castle

118. Windsor.          119. Perthshire.          120. Kincardineshire.

in base, all gold (Fig. 120). The castle is that of Dunnottar, where the 'Honours of Scotland'—the Crown, Sword and Sceptre—were placed for safe-keeping during the Civil War. When the castle was besieged by Parliamentary forces the regalia was smuggled out by the wife of the Minister of Kinneff, who carried the Crown under her apron while her servant bore the sword and sceptre hidden in a bundle of flax. The Honours were concealed under the floor of Kinneff Kirk, and at the restoration of Charles II they were replaced in Edinburgh Castle, where they may still be seen.

The arms of Hereford are also a reminder of the Civil War. The City's original shield was red with three silver lions passant gardant, based on the English Royal Arms. In 1645 it was held for the King against an army of Scots under Leslie, Earl of Leven, and in token of the City's 'singular constancy and resolution' it was granted as an addition to its arms a bordure azure charged with ten silver saltires of St Andrew, representing the besieging Scots. It also received as a crest a silver lion holding a sword, and as supporters two silver lions gardant, each with a blue collar charged with three gold buckles from the arms of Leslie (Fig. 121). The motto may be translated as 'the reward of faithfulness unconquered'.

Monmouth, the birthplace of Henry V, has his lion and antelope as supporters of its arms, while Sutton Coldfield's shield is supported by the greyhound and dragon of Henry

121. Hereford.

VIII from whom the town received its charter. In both cases the beasts wear mural crowns (that is, crowns consisting of masonry and battlemented like castle walls) to difference them from the old royal supporters.

Some royal badges are found in the arms of counties and towns. The red rose of the Lancastrian House occurs in the heraldry of many places in Lancashire, and is the principal feature in the arms of that County: Gules, three gold piles, the middle one reversed, and on each a red rose (Fig. 122). Similarly the white rose of York is frequently seen in the arms of Yorkshire towns. The West Riding County Council bears it within the sun's rays as it was used by Edward IV, the shield being, Ermine, a white rose en soleil and on a chief gules three roses argent (Fig. 123). Northamptonshire shows in its arms associations with both York and Lancaster. The castle of Fotheringay was held by the Dukes of York and by Edward, Earl of March, who became Edward IV. At Grafton Edward married Elizabeth Woodville, a member of a Northamptonshire family which had supported the Lancastrian party. The County shield is argent charged with a red rose of Lancaster and on a chief gules a gold fetterlock (a

122. Lancashire.        123. West Riding        124. Northampton-
                           of Yorkshire.               shire.

badge of the Dukes of York) between two white roses of York
(Fig. 124).

The combined red and white rose of the Tudor sovereigns
occurs in the arms of several places having historic associations with them. Derbyshire has a Tudor rose on a gold
shield, with a chief sable charged with three silver stags'
faces and antlers from the arms of the Cavendish Dukes of
Devonshire, great landowners in the County.

Some counties have in their arms emblems associated with
the kingdoms into which England was divided in Saxon
times. Kent has on its red shield a white rampant horse,
which was the standard of the invaders whose leader was
called Horsa after the tribal emblem. Several towns in Kent
have the horse in their arms. Essex bears on a red shield
three seaxes (or notched swords) with silver blades and gold
hilts, said to have been the weapons of the Saxons (Fig. 125).
Middlesex also has three seaxes on red together with a
Saxon crown, and seaxes occur in the heraldry of many towns
in both counties. The standard of the kingdom of Wessex
was a dragon, and three counties have it in their heraldry.
Somerset bears on a gold shield a red dragon holding a blue
mace—a symbol of local government (Fig. 126). Wiltshire's
shield is barred with eight pieces white and green, representing the chalk downs and the pasture lands, and has a red
dragon on a white canton, while Dorset's supporters are

125. Essex.          126. Somerset.          127. Chester.

two gold dragons each with a red Saxon crown round its neck.

Martlets, derived from the swallows (*hirondelles*) playing on the name of Arundel, have long been regarded as the emblem of Sussex. East Sussex has a Saxon crown and six martlets, all gold, on a red shield, while West Sussex bears six martlets gold on blue with a gold chief. Brighton, Hove, Bexhill and other Sussex towns have martlets in their arms with other emblems.

Cheshire bears the three gold wheatsheaves on blue of the Earls of Chester (Fig. 26) with the addition of a gold sword representing the authority they wielded, while the shield of the City of Chester consists of the arms of England dimidiating those of the earldom (Fig. 127). The silver bear and ragged staff, the famous badge of the Earls of Warwick, appears on a red shield in the arms of Warwickshire with a gold chief charged with three red cross-crosslets from the Beauchamp arms (Fig. 128). Buckinghamshire displays on a shield parted palewise gules and sable a white swan with a gold collar and chain which was a badge of the Earls of Buckingham, derived (like that of Henry IV and Henry V) from the Bohun family; together with a gold chief charged with a green roundle bearing a representation of Whyteleafe Cross in white (Fig. 129). The swan is also found in the arms of the towns of Buckingham, High Wycombe and Slough. The arms of some great feudal families which held lands in

128. Warwick-          129. Buckingham-          130. Lindsey,
     shire.                  shire.               Lincolnshire.

different parts of the country are found in the heraldry of
widely scattered places. The Warenne Earls of Surrey and
Sussex also held lordships in Yorkshire and Lincolnshire, and
we find their gold and blue chequers in the arms not only of
Lewes, Hove, Reigate, Lambeth and Wandsworth, but also
in those of Dewsbury, Halifax, Grantham and Stamford.
Similarly the three red chevronels of Clare are found in the
heraldry of Gloucestershire, Glamorgan, Hertford, Ton-
bridge, and Weymouth.

As in the case of London, many towns have in their arms
the emblem of the patron saint of the principal church. For instance, the shield of Kings Lynn contains three dragons' heads
each pierced by a cross-crosslet, gold on blue, alluding to the
legend of St Margaret who overcame the devil in the form
of a dragon. Peterborough's arms contain the two crossed
keys of St Peter. St Mary the Virgin formed the crest of St
Marylebone and now appears in the arms of the enlarged
City of Westminster which includes St Marylebone.

Ships, anchors and other emblems of the sea are found in
the arms of many places on the coast or on navigable rivers.
Lindsey County Council (Lincolnshire) has a gold viking
ship on barry wavy argent and azure (representing the sea)
and on a blue chief a bull's face and horns in proper colours
between two gold wheatsheaves standing for agriculture
(Fig. 130). In the crest are two human arms, the hands

131. Southampton.

grasping a chain, which, with the motto, 'Service links all,'
refer to 'Lincs.'—the contracted form of the name of the
County. Exmouth has on a silver shield two red anchors
crossed between four blue fish, and on a blue chief ten ancient
ships of silver, representing the ships which the town contributed to Edward III's fleet in 1346. While many ports
have ancient ships of various periods in their arms, more
modern types of vessel are also found in civic heraldry. For
example, Barrow-in-Furness has a paddle-wheel steamship
under steam and sail, and Seaham has a modern cargo
vessel in its arms. In the armorial bearings of Southampton
the two gold lions supporting the shield stand on the sterns
of two ships with the cross of St George flying at the mast-
heads. The arms are, Parted fesswise argent and gules, three
roses counterchanged; and the crest is the figure of Justice
in a gold crown and a purple robe rising from a gold tower
(Fig. 131).

Rivers are represented in many county and town shields.
In the arms of Cambridgeshire the River Cam is shown by a
gold wavy bend on blue, which is surrounded by the gold
flory tressure from the Scottish Royal Arms because the
County was part of the Earldom of Huntingdon, which was
held in the twelfth century by David I, King of Scotland

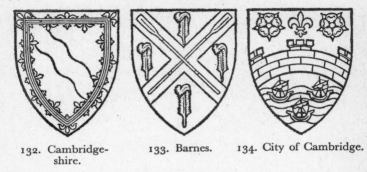

132. Cambridge-          133. Barnes.          134. City of Cambridge.
      shire.

(Fig. 132). Many Thames-side towns have emblems of the
river in their arms. Barnes, which sees the finish of the University Boat Race, has on a blue shield a gold saltire between
four white ostrich feathers, and on the saltire two crossed
oars, one with a dark blue and the other with a light blue
blade (Fig. 133). The ostrich feathers allude to the fact that
the Duke of Windsor (who was Prince of Wales when the
arms were granted in 1932) is a native of Barnes, having been
born at White Lodge, Richmond Park.

Bridges are found in the arms of several towns. The shield
of the City of Cambridge is gules, the base barry wavy argent
and azure and thereon three ships sable, in fess an arched
and turreted bridge of gold, and in chief a gold fleur-de-lis
between two white roses (Fig. 134). A silver fortified bridge
forms the crest, and the supporters are two red sea-horses
with gold fins and tails in proper colours.

The arms of Kesteven County Council (Lincolnshire)
consist of a green shield with an ermine pale, charged with
an uprooted oaktree, standing for the ancient road called
Ermine Street. The shield is supported by a Roman soldier
and a Lincolnshire poacher, and the crest is a heron with a
pike in its beak, referring to the fen country (Fig. 135). The
southern section of Ermine Street is represented by an ermine
pale in the arms of Cheshunt.

The arms of many towns contain emblems referring to the

135. Kesteven, Lincolnshire.

principal industries by which the citizens live. Such charges as woolpacks and fleeces, shuttles and sprigs of cotton, picks, spades and miners' lamps, and hammers and anvils are common in the heraldry of industrial towns. Kettering has a hide representing the manufacture of boots and shoes. Widnes, where there are chemical works, has an alembic—a vessel used in distilling. In the arms of Rugby a thunderbolt stands for electrical undertakings. Stoke-on-Trent, in the Potteries, has the Portland vase in its arms and a potter of ancient Egypt as its crest. Paper manufacture is represented in the arms of Bury by the papyrus plant and in those of Farnworth by hornets—nature's paper-makers. The training of horses, and the most famous horse-race—the Derby—are represented in the arms of Epsom and Ewell: Parted chevronwise vert and argent, in chief two gold horses' heads and in base two bars wavy azure, with the motto 'None such' referring to the old royal palace of Nonsuch (Fig. 136). Newmarket has a running horse in its shield.

Railways are referred to by George Stephenson's 'Locomotion No. 1' in the shield of Darlington and by an engine of a more modern type in that of Swindon, while Crewe has in its arms a wheel with six spokes, representing the six rail-

K

way lines radiating from its station. Several towns display wings in allusion to local airports. Hendon has a winged airscrew as its crest, and Beddington-and-Wallington has an aeroplane as a charge on its shield. This is an instance of how heraldry is able to keep up to date by adopting as charges things which were undreamed of when it began.

Allusions to the names of towns are common in civic heraldry. To select a few instances from many, Barrow-in-Furness has a bee and an arrow, Beverley a beaver, Cowbridge a cow on a bridge, Gateshead a goat's head and gate, the Isle of Ely County Council an eel, and Oxford an ox fording a stream. Sometimes the motto plays on the name of the town, for example: *Reddite Deo* ('Render unto God') is the motto of Redditch; and *Spe nemo ruet* ('With hope, no one shall fail') is that of Spennymoor. In the case of Chichester Rural District, the name is hidden in the motto, *Adhuc hic hesterna* ('The things of yesterday are still with us').

The arms of some towns contain emblems referring to important historical events which took place there. For example, the shield of Battle Rural District contains a sword referring to the battle of Hastings and is accompanied by the motto, *Per bellum patria* ('Through battle came the country'). The sealing of Magna Carta at Runnymede is commemorated in the shield of Egham by King John's crown and a representation of the Charter all in proper colours on a green field (Fig. 137). East Barnet's arms, containing crossed swords between a red rose and a white rose, record the battle of Barnet in the Wars of the Roses. Richard III's death at the Battle of Bosworth is recalled by the crest of Market Bosworth consisting of a white boar, which was Richard's badge, pierced by a sword with a silver blade and a blue hilt, silver and blue being the colours of the House of Lancaster. Chesterfield has as supporters of its shield a cock and a pynot (or magpie) recalling the meeting of the Earl of Devonshire, the Earl of Danby and others, at the Cock and Pynot Inn, Whittington, which led to the overthrow of James II and the 'Glorious Revolution' of 1688. Sometimes

136. Epsom and        137. Egham.        138. Dursley.
Ewell.

remarkable incidents in local history are recorded. For instance, the crest of Bungay (Suffolk) consists of 'the Black
Dog of Bungay courant proper upon a ray of lightning fesswise gules'. This refers to a tradition, recorded in the
Churchwardens' Book, that on a Sunday morning in August
1577, during a terrific thunderstorm, a black dog, 'or the
divel in such a likeness', appeared in the church, and in the
words of an old rhyme:

> All down the church in midst of fire
> The hellish monster flew,
> And passing onwards to the quire
> He many people slew.

Famous people born in or associated with the county or
town are sometimes commemorated in the local heraldry.
Warwickshire uses Shakespeare's motto, *Non sanz droict* ('Not
without right'), and Devon that of Sir Francis Drake,
*Auxilio Divino* ('By Divine assistance'). A nightingale in the
arms of Ystradgynlais (Breconshire) refers to Madame Patti,
who was born there. The arms of Dursley Rural District
Council, in Gloucestershire, contain the Holy Bible, commemorating its translator, William Tyndale, who was born
in the district. The arms are, Gules, a Holy Lamb proper
within an orle of crosses formy argent, and on a chief vert an

open book proper bound in gold and bearing the words
HOLY BIBLE in letters sable, between two gold cart-
wheels each with eight spokes (Fig. 138). The Lamb (which
carries a flag charged with a red cross) refers to the Gloucestershire wool industry, and the crosses are from the arms of
the Berkeleys, Viscounts Dursley. One of the wheels alludes
to local engineering works, and the other commemorates Sir
Isaac Pitman, who began teaching his system of shorthand at
Dursley, basing its symbols on the spokes and curves of a
wheel. The crest (not here illustrated) is a white-fronted
goose on a mound of sand in a gold crown consisting of
palisades, and refers to the Severn Wildfowl Trust.

In so short a space it is possible to give only a brief account
of a few of the many arms of cities, counties and towns in
Great Britain. Those who are interested in this branch of
heraldry should be able to discover the arms of the place
where they live by calling at the town hall or public offices,
or at the local library. A book on Civic Heraldry is mentioned
in the list of books at the end of this volume.

Since the first edition of this book, some of the places
mentioned in this chapter have been affected by local
government changes. Barnes is now part of the new borough
of Richmond-on-Thames, Hendon has been merged with
Barnet, and Beddington and Wallington form part of Sutton.
Cambridgeshire and the Isle of Ely now form one county.
The London County Council has been replaced by the
Greater London Council, which has as arms: *Barry wavy of
six argent and azure, on a chief gules a gold Saxon crown.*

139. Westminster Bank.

140. Martins Bank.

141. Prudential Assurance Company.

# 10. Heraldry in Everyday Life

PEOPLE who become interested in heraldry naturally begin to notice the arms, crests and badges which hitherto they may have passed by with no more than a glance. They discover that much heraldic insignia is to be seen not only in churches and historic buildings but also in less likely places. In many towns you will see arms displayed outside banks and insurance company offices, and in London and the great provincial cities you may see them on the premises of important corporations. If you travel by rail you will find the badge of British Railways on locomotives and rolling stock, and if you go by road you will often notice the arms of the counties or towns through which you pass set up on a sign at their boundaries. Both in town and country you will see armorial bearings on the signs of many hotels and inns. All this goes to show that the ancient art of heraldry is still very much alive. Its use is not restricted to people of high rank or families of a certain standing. The bearing of arms by all sorts of corporate bodies has resulted in heraldry coming into touch with everyday life at many points. A few instances of such arms are given below.

Westminster Bank frequently displays its arms outside its

branches. These are, Azure, a fess wavy argent between ten white roses, their seeds and sepals or, and in the dexter chief a gold portcullis (Fig. 139). The portcullis has a double significance, being an emblem of security and also the principal charge in the shield of the City of Westminster. The wavy fess stands for the River Thames and the roses represent the several banking businesses which have been merged to form Westminster Bank. Barclays Bank, developed from a business carried on in the eighteenth century at the sign of 'The Black Spread Eagle' in Lombard Street, London, still uses a black eagle as a device, while Lloyds Bank uses a black horse, which is also derived from a former sign. Two banks combine on their shields emblems denoting business activities in London and a provincial city. The Midland Bank displays the arms of Birmingham with the addition of a sword from the shield of the City of London. Martins Bank bears on a gold shield a black liver-bird (or cormorant) with a strip of laver (seaweed) in its beak, from the arms of Liverpool, and on a green chief a gold grasshopper, from the one which surmounts London's Royal Exchange (Fig. 140). The grasshopper was the crest of Sir Thomas Gresham, founder of the Royal Exchange.

The arms of the Prudential Assurance Company, which are often shown outside their premises, are, Sable, three bars embattled or between two flanches argent each charged with three martlets gules (Fig. 141. The *flanches* are the sides of the shield enclosed by the curved lines.). The crest is a female figure representing Prudence. The bars stand for Holborn Bars, at the boundary of the City of London, where the Prudential have their main offices. They are embattled as a symbol of protection by assurance. The martlets are from the arms of the Furnival family whose town house, Furnival's Inn, formerly stood on the site. The Pearl Assurance Company has in its arms a saltire from the shield of Holborn, a sword for London, and emblems of the parishes of St Giles and Stepney, with which it has associations. Lloyd's Corporation, famous in the field of marine insurance, has a shield

142. Royal Mail Lines.

parted fesswise, in chief the arms of the City of London and the base azure with a gold anchor with a cable twisted round it. The supporters are heraldic sea-lions each holding a trident, and the crest is H.M.S. *La Lutine* in full sail. This ship was wrecked off the coast of Holland in 1799 when carrying bullion to Hamburg. Her bell was recovered and hangs at Lloyd's, where it is struck on the occasion of important announcements. Lloyd's motto is *Fidentia* ('Confidence').

Among shipping companies, Royal Mail Lines have as arms, Azure, on waves of the sea proper a ship in full sail or, the sails argent, flying from each mast a pennon argent charged with a saltire gules; upon a chief argent a saltire gules charged with the Royal Crown proper. The design of the chief is the house flag of the line. A similar ship but having red saltires on the sails forms the crest, and the supporters are two sea-horses proper (Fig. 142).

The arms of British European Airways are, Argent, a fess between three astral crowns gules (Fig. 143). An astral

143. British European
Airways.

144. Badge of British
Railways.

crown has a rim set with four stars each between a pair of
wings.

In the days when there were separate railway companies
serving different parts of Great Britain several of them had
armorial bearings, while others used heraldic devices incorporating the shields of the principal cities on their lines. Today arms are borne for the railways generally by the British
Transport Commission. These are: Vert, a fess double
cotised argent, in chief three railway wheels also argent and
in base a silver portcullis with gold chains, and on the fess
two barrulets (narrow bars) wavy azure. The crest is a demi-
lion gules holding between the forepaws a silver railway-
wheel, and the supporters are two lions gardant each charged
on the shoulder with a railway-wheel. 'Double cotised' means
that the fess is placed between two pairs of very narrow bars.
These represent railway lines, while the wavy barrulets on
the fess stand for canals. The portcullis is from the arms of
the City of Westminster, where the Commission has its headquarters. The Commission also has a badge which consists of
a red demi-lion holding a silver railway wheel, like the one
in the crest but rising from a coronet composed of oak-leaves,
roses, thistles and leeks for the various parts of Great Britain.

145. United Kingdom Atomic Energy Authority.

This badge appears on British Railways rolling-stock (Fig. 144).

If you pass through Paddington Station, London, you should make a point of looking at the colourful display of heraldry by the gates to the departure platforms. This consists of the arms of the counties and principal towns served by lines from Paddington.

The armorial bearings of the United Kingdom Atomic Energy Authority show how the traditional forms of heraldry can be used to illustrate modern scientific developments. The arms are: Sable, semy of roundles argent, a pile barry dancetty gold and gules; crest, on a wreath argent and sable a sun charged with a martlet sable within a voided escutcheon gules (that is, the centre of the escutcheon is cut out so that the sun shows through it); supporters, two pantheons gules each semy of fifteen gold molets, thirteen with six points and two with seven points, and having about the neck a gold palisado crown with a gold chain affixed thereto and turned over the creature's back (Fig. 145). The Authority also has a badge consisting of a lion passant gardant gules supporting with its right forepaw a pile sable. The motto is, *E Minimis Maxima* ('Out of the least the greatest'). The black field with white roundles represents the atomic pile, a rectangular block of graphite into which many uranium rods have been inserted. The heraldic pile barry dancetty symbolizes nuclear fission taking place within the atomic pile and generating atomic energy. In the crest, the sun, as a symbol of heat and energy, is charged with emblems from the arms of Lord Rutherford, the pioneer of atomic research. The pantheon is a rare heraldic creature always shown spangled with stars, and here refers to the natural forces in the universe, while the crowns composed of palisades, and the chains, show that the powers are controlled. If you add up the points of the stars on each pantheon you will find that they number ninety-two, corresponding to the number of electrons in uranium.

Scientific and technical ideas are also expressed in the arms of some of the professional societies. For example, the shield of the Institution of Civil Engineers is, Or, on a pale azure between two annulets sable, a gold thunderbolt between in chief the sun in splendour or and in base a roundle barry wavy argent and azure (Fig. 147). Here the sun stands for light and heat, the thunderbolt for electrical power, the blue and white roundle for water, and the annulets for metals. The charges thus represent the great forces in nature which are directed by the civil engineer to the use and benefit of mankind.

The Royal Society of Health has a blue shield charged with a roundle barry wavy argent and azure within golden rays, representing the essentials of health—a clean atmosphere,

146. British Limbless Ex-Servicemen's
Association.

pure water, and sunshine. This is supported by Hygeia, the
goddess of health, and by a stork, here used as an emblem of
maternity and child welfare. The crest is an apple tree bearing seven apples, recalling the saying 'An apple a day keeps
the doctor away', and thus standing for preventive medicine.

Figure 146 illustrates the arms of the British Limbless Ex-
Servicemen's Association. The shield is blue and is charged
with a gold sun on which is a cross potent parted saltirewise,
the vertical limbs being blue and the horizontal ones red.
This form of cross is called 'potent' from an old word for a
crutch because it has crutch-shaped ends. It was formerly a
crusading emblem, and was chosen by the Association as a
suitable symbol for men disabled in a righteous cause. Its

blue limbs stand for the Royal Navy and Royal Air Force
and its red limbs for the Army and Royal Marines. The cross
has the 'place in the sun' the Association aims to give its
members. The crest also refers to the four services. The lions
supporting the shield are seated, referring to the fact that
many members are necessarily sedentary through disable-
ment. The dexter lion is gold (like the English lion) and has on
its collar roses for England and a daffodil for Wales, while
the sinister one is red (the colour of the Scottish lion) and has
on the collar thistles and shamrock.

The arms of The Times Publishing Company represent
the newspaper press in heraldic form. They are: Argent,
eight barrulets sable and over all a gold caduceus (Fig. 148).
The black barrulets on white suggest a column of print, and
the caduceus—a winged staff entwined by serpents—is the
rod of Mercury, the messenger of the gods. A banner bearing
these arms may often be seen flying over *The Times* office in
London, but the arms do not appear on copies of this newspaper. Instead *The Times*, in common with some other news-
papers, displays the Royal Arms at the head of each issue.
This is no doubt a sign of loyalty, but there does not appear
to be any authority for it.

Since one of the earliest uses of heraldry was to distinguish
competitors in tournaments, which were the sporting events
of medieval knighthood, it is interesting and appropriate
that it is used in this way at the present time, though now it
is not the individual player but the team which is identified
by arms and badges. Men who represent England in Association Football wear on their shirts and caps the arms of the
Football Association, which are, Argent, semy of Tudor
roses proper, three lions passant gardant in pale azure (Fig.
149). Welsh international players wear the arms of the Football Association of Wales: Ermine, a dragon gules within a
bordure vert charged with eleven leeks or. A shamrock is
used as a badge by the Irish Football Association, while that
of Scotland has a device incorporating a football, crossed
pennons and a thistle supported by lions. A number of local

147. Institution of
Civil Engineers.

148. The Times
Publishing Company.

149. Football
Association.

clubs use a version of the arms of their home town, or some
emblem of their own devising—for instance, Tottenham Hot-
spurs have a black cock and Arsenal a gun.

The national rose, thistle and shamrock are used in Rugby
football for players for England, Scotland and Ireland, while
Welsh internationals use the badge of the three ostrich
feathers associated with the Prince of Wales.

Men who play cricket for England in this country have a
badge consisting of three white lions (not placed on a shield)
with the Royal Crown above them, but those who represent
England in Test Matches abroad use the device of St George
and the Dragon. Many county cricket clubs use the arms or
part of the arms of their county.

The custom of using heraldic signs outside inns is very
ancient and probably began in various ways. Some noblemen
when travelling had escutcheons bearing their arms hung outside the place where they lodged, and if this was an inn the
innkeeper might beg to be allowed to retain the escutcheon
as a memento of a great man's visit, and it became the sign
of the hostelry. In the days when retainers of kings and nobles
wore their badges, a retainer setting up as an innkeeper
might have displayed his lord's badge outside the house as a
token of his patronage. Some may have exhibited one of the
royal badges as a sign of loyalty to the crown. Among the
signs and names of inns derived from one of the royal badges

we find the *Falcon* of the Plantagenets; the *Rose*, and the *Rose and Crown*, which may come from Lancaster, York or Tudor according to the colour of the rose; the *White Hart* of Richard II; the *Swan and Antelope* of the Lancastrian kings; the *Sun and Rose* of York; the *White Lion* of March; the *Black Bull* of Clarence; and the *Red Dragon* and *Greyhound* of the Tudors. However, you must not assume that every inn with one of these signs dates from Plantagenet or Tudor times. Some of them certainly do so, but these names and signs have become generally popular and have been adopted by many modern inns.

Among inn signs which originated in the badges of great nobles are the *Bear and Ragged Staff* of the Earls of Warwick, and the *Talbot* of the Earls of Shrewsbury. Sometimes a crest is used as an inn sign, as in the case of the *Eagle and Child*, from the crest of the Earls of Derby, consisting of an eagle standing over a baby in swaddling clothes. This commemorates the legend of an ancestor who in infancy was saved from being carried off by an eagle. Where you find an ancient inn with the name and sign of the *Chequers*, and it shows a shield checky gold and azure, this may possibly be derived from the arms of the Warenne Earls of Arundel, but in some cases an inn of this name bears a sign which is not heraldic but consists of a chess or draughts board.

A number of inns called the *Lion* or *Golden Lion*, or the *Unicorn*, derive their name and sign from the Royal Supporters. The *King's Arms* is a popular name and where it has an heraldic sign this should show some historic version of the Royal Arms because it is not permissible for an inn to display the present Royal Arms. The *Star and Garter* is an instance of a name and sign derived from the insignia of an order of chivalry.

A very large number of inns have on their signs the arms of some important local family. In some cases the family has died out or has moved away from the district, and their arms outside the inn, and perhaps monuments in the church, are the only traces of their former standing in the neighbour-

150. Heraldic Inn-sign.

151. Heraldic Milestone.

hood. In recent years the owners of many inns have shown great interest in their signs and have commissioned experts to repaint them, with the result that many of them are fine examples of heraldic art. Fig. 150 shows the sign of The Lane Arms at Bentley. These arms are described in Chapter 5.

Occasionally you will see arms or badges on old boundary-posts and milestones. Fig. 151 shows a milestone on the Trumpington Road, Cambridge. The arms are those of Trinity Hall impaling those of Dr Mowse, a former Master of the College, who left funds which were applied to the provision of milestones on the Cambridge to London road early in the eighteenth century. These are said to have been the first milestones set up in Britain since Roman times.

Many people possessing arms display them on the book-

152. Book-plate of The Right
Hon. W. E. Gladstone.

153. Heraldic design on
a Christmas card.

plates which they paste inside the volumes in their library as
a mark of ownership. You will often find such plates in old
books. Armorial book-plates can be interesting examples of
the heraldic art of the period when they were drawn. Many
of them contain examples of quartered arms, and some include insignia of rank or membership of an order of chivalry.
Fig. 152 shows the book-plate of the Rt. Hon. W. E. Gladstone, M.P., presented to him on his golden wedding anni-
versary in 1889 by Lord Northbourne. Here the arms are
accompanied by three kites, or *gleds*, the one at the bottom
standing on *stones*, forming a play on the name Gladstone.

Heraldry is also sometimes used on Christmas cards. Fig.
153 is an example. The little figure standing in the ship
indicates that the card is that of an officer of arms. His arms
appear on the sail and those of his wife on the banner, while
the swan at the prow is his crest.

# 11. The Heralds and State Pageantry

THE English kings of arms, heralds and pursuivants first acquired a London house, in which to keep their books and records, in 1484, when they were incorporated by a charter granted by Richard III. Unfortunately this house was taken away in the following year, when Henry VII annulled the grants made by his predecessor. For the next seventy years the officers of arms had no headquarters, and during this period many of their records passed into private hands. In 1555 Queen Mary gave them a new charter, together with Derby House in the City of London. Here the heralds established their library and records, and in the course of time they obtained by gift or purchase many of the books and documents which had formerly been dispersed. Derby House was destroyed in the Great Fire of 1666, but most of the records and manuscripts were saved. The present College of Arms (or Heralds' College), in Queen Victoria Street, was built on the site of the former house between 1670 and 1690. It is a building of time-darkened red brick forming three sides of a quadrangle with fine ornamental gates and railings along the fourth side. A stone stairway leads to a stately panelled hall, hung with banners and with the paintings of former heralds, and containing a high canopied seat carved with the arms of the Duke of Norfolk. This hall is the Earl Marshal's Court where the Court of Chivalry was formerly held. However, on the only occasion in modern times when this Court has met it took place at the Law Courts, where there is greater space and convenience.

Adjoining the hall there is a public office where the officer of arms 'in waiting' (that is, on duty for a week) receives members of the public calling at the College with inquiries or general business. In this central block are the record rooms and libraries, and the office of Garter King of Arms. The other kings, heralds and pursuivants have sets of chambers in the two wings of the building. Here they receive their clients and carry out their professional practice in the spheres of heraldry and genealogy, which include such matters as tracing pedigrees and drawing up family trees, often richly illustrated with heraldry; investigating claims to bear arms, and in suitable cases arranging for the grant of armorial bearings either to individuals or to corporate bodies. They have the assistance of a staff of record-searchers, heraldic artists and scriveners.

By no means all those who seek the services of the heralds are people of rank or title. Many of them are ordinary citizens with no pretensions to nobility, but sufficiently interested in their family background to wish to discover more about it. Some are from the Commonwealth countries or the United States of America, descended from some English family. Similarly those who petition for armorial bearings are not necessarily of knightly or higher rank. The kings of arms (acting under the authority of the Earl Marshal) are prepared to consider an application from any person of integrity on his own merits, and every year a number of men who have shown themselves to be gentlemen in the best sense obtain grants of arms and thereby become 'gentlemen of coat-armour'. As the officers of arms receive only small nominal salaries, they must charge their clients fees for their services, but the fees payable in connection with grants of arms are quite moderate.

The membership of the College of Arms consists of three kings of arms, six heralds and four pursuivants, all of whom have historic titles. They are officers of the Royal Household. Garter is the principal King of Arms in England and, as his name implies, he is the King of Arms of the Order of the Garter. The first Garter was appointed by Henry V in 1415. The other kings of arms are Clarenceux (from the title Clare or Clarence), who has jurisdiction south of the River Trent, and Norroy and Ulster, with authority north of the Trent and in Northern Ireland. The title Norroy is from Norrois—the men of the north country. Until 1943 the offices of Norroy and Ulster were separate.

The heralds are called by historic names associated in some cases with royal dignities and in others with lordships whose private heralds eventually became royal officers. They are York, Lancaster, Richmond, Chester, Windsor and Somerset. The titles of the pursuivants are Bluemantle (from the robe of the Order of the Garter), Rouge Croix (from the cross of St George), Rouge Dragon and Portcullis (from the badges of Henry VII, by whom these offices were created).

In addition to the members of the College of Arms—who are the officers of arms *in ordinary*—additional officers termed *extraordinary* are sometimes appointed. While these are now royal officers, some may also be regarded as a survival of the private heralds of the nobility, because they take their names from the titles held by the Duke of Norfolk, Earl Marshal. The present extraordinary officers are Norfolk Herald, Arundel Herald, Fitzalan Pursuivant and Wales Herald.

In Scotland, Lyon King of Arms is assisted by Albany, Marchmont and Rothesay Heralds, and Dingwall, Unicorn and Carrick Pursuivants. The High Constable of Scotland has a private pursuivant entitled Slains.

On ceremonial occasions the officers of arms wear their tabards over scarlet levée coats with knee-breeches—normally black, but white at a Coronation. The tabards are embroidered with the Royal Arms on front, back and sleeves. The Scottish officers wear tabards of the Royal Arms as used in Scotland, with the Scottish lion in the first and fourth quarters and the English arms in the second quarter.

Garter, as King of Arms of the Order of the Garter, carries a sceptre with a square head topped by the Royal Crown, bearing on one face the cross of St George within the Garter, and on the other the red cross impaling the Royal Arms, which also forms the badge of office which he wears suspended from the collar of SS (Fig. 48). Norroy and Ulster also has a sceptre as King of Arms of the Order of St Patrick. He and

Clarenceux have official badges and wear the collar of SS, as do the heralds. Clarenceux King of Arms and the heralds and pursuivants each carries a white staff of office topped by a blue dove rising from a gold crown, this being the crest of the College of Arms. The heralds and pursuivants also have medallions bearing the Royal Arms which they may wear as a decoration on formal occasions when they are not attired in their tabards.

Garter King of Arms attends in his tabard and conducts the ceremony when a newly-created peer is introduced in the House of Lords. There are usually only two events in the year at which the other officers of arms wear their tabards, namely the State Opening of Parliament by the Queen and the annual service of the Order of the Garter at Windsor. There are other rare occasions when they carry out ceremonial functions, particularly those arising from a change of reign. The procedure followed in 1952 was in accordance with long-standing tradition.

After the death of King George VI the Privy Council, together with representatives of the Commonwealth and other dignitaries, met to draw up the proclamation declaring 'that the High and Mighty Princess Elizabeth Alexandra Mary has now, by the Death of our late Sovereign of Happy Memory, become Queen Elizabeth the Second, by the Grace of God Queen of this Realm and of Her other Realms and Territories, Head of the Commonwealth, Defender of the Faith.' The proclamation (of which the foregoing is a short extract) was read from the balcony of Friary Court, St James's Palace, by Garter King of Arms in the presence of the Earl Marshal and others, attended by the other kings of arms, heralds and pursuivants, and the sergeants at arms. The officers of arms then proceeded in carriages to Trafalgar Square where the proclamation was read by Lancaster Herald at the statue of King Charles I. They then drove to the site of Temple Bar where, in accordance with tradition, a cord had been stretched across the road marking the guarded entrance to the City of London, and the City Marshal in the

presence of the Lord Mayor challenged them with the words
'Who comes here?' A pursuivant alighted from the carriage,
and announced 'Her Majesty's officers of arms, who demand
entrance into the City of London in order to proclaim Her
Royal Majesty Queen Elizabeth the Second'. By order of the
Lord Mayor the heralds were then admitted, and the proclamation was read at the end of Fetter Lane by Norroy and
Ulster King of Arms. Finally, accompanied by the Lord
Mayor and other prominent citizens, the officers of arms
proceeded to the Royal Exchange, where the proclamation
was read a fourth time by Clarenceux King of Arms.

At the same time in Edinburgh the proclamation was read
from the Mercat Cross by the Lord Provost to the citizens, and
again by Lyon King of Arms to the people of Scotland, after
which Lyon read it at the gate of Edinburgh Castle, the
Palace of Holyroodhouse and the Shore of Leith.

The heralds took their place in the cortège at the King's
funeral at Windsor, and in accordance with tradition Garter
King of Arms recited the roll of the late Sovereign's titles
over the open grave.

In connection with the Coronation of the Sovereign, the
duties of the officers of arms were far from being purely
ceremonial. For months before the event the Earl Marshal,
assisted by Garter and several of the other heraldic officers,
was busily engaged on the innumerable and complicated
arrangements which had to be made. On the great day, the
heralds in their tabards were on duty in Westminster Abbey,
acting as escorts to royal personages, while Garter King of
Arms had a direct part in the ceremonies, preceding the
Archbishop of Canterbury and the Great Officers of State in
their progress of the four sides of the space round the Throne,
at each of which the Archbishop presented the Queen to her
subjects, who acclaimed her with the words, 'God save
Queen Elizabeth'. When the crown was placed on the Queen's
head, and the peers and peeresses put on their coronets, the
kings of arms also put on their crowns. The Coronation is
now the only occasion when they wear them.

The ceremonial in connection with the State Opening of
Parliament (which usually takes place in November) is con-
ducted by the Earl Marshal. The kings, heralds and pursuivants of arms are present as officers of the Queen's Household. Wearing their tabards, they attend the Great Officers
of State who, in their robes, receive the Queen at the Royal
Entrance to the Palace of Westminster. The pursuivants and
heralds head the procession into the Royal Gallery, and when
the Queen has put on her robes and the Crown, they lead
the way into the House of Lords, where they form a colourful
group beside the Throne. After the Queen has delivered her
speech, the heraldic officers head the procession back through
the Royal Gallery, and while the Queen unrobes they line
the steps of the Royal Entrance where the state carriage is
waiting. The ceremonial closes with the Sovereign passing
between these officers of her Household attired in her Royal
Arms.

At the annual service of the Order of the Garter the kings,
heralds and pursuivants of arms carry out their most ancient
duties of attending upon knights on an occasion of chivalry,
and marshalling the procession. Garter King of Arms, in
his mantle as an officer of the Order, directs the proceedings. Wearing their tabards the officers of arms assemble
with the Knights of the Garter in St George's Hall at Windsor Castle, where the Queen and the Duke of Edinburgh
join them. Headed by the pursuivants and heralds, the
procession passes down the stairs to the Grand Entrance,
where the Military Knights of Windsor are formed up,
through the Norman Gate and the Middle and Lower Wards
of the Castle, where those privileged to view it are gathered.
It enters St George's Chapel by the West Door. The Sovereign and the Knights of the Order go to their stalls, and
the pursuivants and heralds take up their positions in the
chancel; they remain standing throughout the service. At its
close the officers of arms take up positions on the steps to the
West Door where they are joined by the Knights of the
Garter, and the Queen, led by the hand by the Duke of

Edinburgh, passes to her car through a scene of historic pageantry.

Lyon King of Arms and the Scottish heralds and pursuivants participate in a similar way when a service of the Order of the Thistle is held at St Giles's, Edinburgh. The Orders of the Bath, St Michael and St George, and the British Empire, have each a King of Arms, but these are not members of the College of Arms and do not wear tabards.

# How to Study Heraldry

IF THIS short account of heraldry has so interested you that you wish to know more about it, there are a number of books which you will find useful, some of which are not too expensive to buy while others will probably be found in a public library. However, heraldry should be studied not only from books, but also from actual examples of armorial bearings, ancient and modern, which may come to your notice. When you observe a coat of arms study it carefully and see whether you can tell something about the person or body it stands for. Try to blazon the arms for yourself. A Peerage and Baronetage in which arms are both illustrated and described in heraldic terms will enable you to practise on the one hand blazoning, and on the other sketching arms from a blazon. It will also give you many examples of heraldic forms and charges, of quartered shields, of crests and supporters, and of the various coronets and helms.

It will help you to become familiar with heraldic terms if you colour the illustrations in this book, using the descriptions of arms as a guide. The tinctures of heraldry are not exact shades, but strong, bright colours should be used such as vermilion for gules, ultramarine mixed with a little white for azure, and Hooker's green (or a mixture of Prussian blue and gamboge) for vert. In some of the illustrations the sable parts are already filled in but where this has not been done they should be coloured black. However, in the case of animals or birds which are blazoned as sable it is better to paint them a dark grey and shade them with black. Similarly, creatures described as argent may be shaded with light grey, but otherwise the white paper will stand for argent without painting it. Gold should be represented by a good yellow, such as chrome, cadmium or aureolin.

When you have an opportunity, visit Westminster Abbey, or Canterbury Cathedral, or St George's Chapel at Windsor, or some other ancient building where there are examples of heraldry of all periods, and see whether there are any heraldic manuscripts or other exhibits in your local museum. Go to your county offices or town hall and find out what are the arms of your county or the place where you live, and if possible what they mean. In short, take every possible opportunity of looking at heraldry, and use books chiefly to discover the explanation of what you see.

Out of many books on the subject I select the following as likely to be most useful for your purpose:

*Simple Heraldry*, by Iain Moncrieffe, amusingly illustrated in colour. (Thomas Nelson and Sons, Ltd.)

*Heraldry in England*, by Anthony Wagner (King Penguin).

*The Romance of Heraldry*, by C. W. Scott-Giles (4th reprint 1964, J. M. Dent and Sons Ltd.).

*Boutell's Heraldry*, edited by C. W. Scott-Giles and J. P. Brooke-Little (latest edition 1966, Frederick Warne and Co. Ltd.).

*A Grammar of English Heraldry*, by W. H. St John Hope (2nd edition revised by Anthony Wagner, Cambridge University Press).

*The Colour of Heraldry*—thirty-two heraldic effigies in colour (The Heraldry Society).

*Royal Beasts*, by H. Stanford London (The Heraldry Society).

*The Siege of Caerlaverock*—an illustrated translation of a fourteenth-century rime describing the arms of those present at the siege in 1300 (The Heraldry Society).

*Civic Heraldry of England and Wales*, by C. W. Scott-Giles (2nd edition 1953, J. M. Dent and Sons Ltd.).

*The Coat of Arms* (quarterly) and other publications of the Heraldry Society, some of which have been specially prepared for newcomers to the subject.

The Heraldry Society (Hon. Secretary, 59 Gordon Square, London, W.C.1) is open to all who are interested in heraldry. Fellowship is restricted to persons who have made some notable contribution to the subject, but anyone can join as a member, and there is an associate section for juniors.

# INDEX

160